W9-CHY-870

In a Reading State of
MIND

Brain Research, Teacher Modeling, and Comprehension Instruction

Douglas Fisher   Nancy Frey   Diane Lapp

INTERNATIONAL
Reading Association
800 BARKSDALE ROAD, PO BOX 8139
NEWARK, DE 19714-8139, USA
www.reading.org

The International Reading Association attempts, through its publications, to provide a forum for a wide spectrum of opinions on reading. This policy permits divergent viewpoints without implying the endorsement of the Association.

Executive Editor, Books   Corinne M. Mooney
Developmental Editor   Charlene M. Nichols
Developmental Editor   Tori Mello Bachman
Developmental Editor   Stacey L. Reid
Editorial Production Manager   Shannon T. Fortner
Design and Composition Manager   Anette Schuetz

Project Editors   Tori Mello Bachman and Wesley Ford

Cover   Illustration and design by Snyder Creative

Library of Congress Cataloging-in-Publication Data
Fisher, Douglas, 1965-
  In a reading state of mind : brain research, teacher modeling, and
comprehension instruction / Douglas Fisher, Nancy Frey, and Diane Lapp.
      p. cm.
  Includes bibliographical references and index.
  ISBN 978-0-87207-777-5
  1. Reading comprehension--Study and teaching. 2. Reading, Psychology
of. 3. Critical thinking--Study and teaching. I. Frey, Nancy, 1959-
II. Lapp, Diane. III. Title.
  LB1050.45.F57 2008
  428.4'3--dc22
                                                                2008035946

CONTENTS

Douglas Fisher, PhD, is Professor of Language and Literacy Education in the Department of Teacher Education at San Diego State University (SDSU; San Diego, California, USA) and a classroom teacher at Health Sciences High & Middle College (HSHMC; San Diego, California, USA). He is the recipient of an International Reading Association (IRA) Celebrate Literacy Award, the Farmer Award for excellence in writing from the National Council of Teachers of English, as well as a Christa McAuliffe Award for excellence in teacher education from the American Association of State Colleges and Universities. He was the chair of IRA's Adolescent Literacy Committee. Doug has published numerous articles on reading and literacy, differentiated instruction, and curriculum design as well as books such as *Creating Literacy-Rich Schools for Adolescents* (with Gay Ivey), *Better Learning Through Structured Teaching: A Framework for the Gradual Release of Responsibility* (with Nancy Frey), and *Teaching English Language Learners: A Differentiated Approach* (with Carol Rothenberg). He has taught a variety of courses in SDSU's teacher-credentialing program as well as graduate-level courses on English language development and literacy. An early intervention specialist and language development specialist, he has taught high school English, writing, and literacy development to public school students. He can be reached at dfisher@mail.sdsu.edu.

Nancy Frey, PhD, is Professor of Literacy in the School of Teacher Education at SDSU and a classroom teacher at HSHMC. Before moving to San Diego, Nancy was a special education teacher in the Broward County (FL) Public Schools, where she taught students at the elementary and middle school level. She is a recipient of the Christa McAuliffe Award for excellence in teacher education from the American Association of State Colleges and Universities. Nancy was the chair of IRA's Media Awards Committee. Her research interests include reading and literacy, assessment, intervention, and curriculum design, and she was a finalist for IRA's Outstanding Dissertation Award. She has published in *The Reading Teacher, Journal of Adolescent & Adult Literacy, English Journal, Voices From the Middle, Middle School Journal, Remedial and Special Education, Educational Leadership,* and *California English.* She has coauthored books on literacy such as *Improving Adolescent Literacy: Strategies at Work, Reading for Information in Elementary School: Content Literacy Strategies to Build Comprehension, Scaffolded Writing Instruction: Teaching With a Gradual-Release Framework,* and *Checking for Understanding: Formative Assessment Techniques for Your Classroom* (all with Douglas Fisher). She teaches a variety of courses in SDSU's teacher-credentialing program on elementary and secondary reading instruction and literacy in content areas, classroom management, and supporting students with diverse learning needs. She can be reached at nfrey@mail.sdsu.edu.

Diane Lapp, EdD, Distinguished Professor of Education in the Department of Teacher Education at SDSU, has taught in elementary and middle schools, and most recently is teaching English at HSHMC. Her major areas of research and instruction have centered on struggling readers and their families who live in urban, economically poor settings. Diane directs and teaches field-based preservice and graduate programs and courses. She was the coeditor of California's literacy journal *The California Reader.* She also has authored, coauthored, and edited many articles, columns, texts, handbooks, and children's materials on reading and language arts, including the following: *Teaching Reading to Every Child,* a reading methods textbook in its fourth edition; *Content Area Reading and Learning: Instructional Strategies; Accommodating Differences Among English Language Learners: 75 Literacy Lessons; Handbook of Research on Teaching the English Language Arts,* and *Handbook of Research on Teaching Literacy Through the Communicative and Visual Arts* (Vol. 1 & 2). She has also chaired and cochaired several IRA and National Reading Council committees, and she is currently the chair of IRA's Early Literacy Committee. Her many educational awards include being named Outstanding Teacher Educator and Faculty Member in the

Department of Teacher Education at SDSU, the Distinguished Research Lecturer from SDSU's Graduate Division of Research, and IRA's 1996 Outstanding Teacher Educator of the Year. Diane is also a member of both the California and the IRA Reading Halls of Fame. She can be reached at lapp@mail.sdsu.edu.

CHAPTER 1

If You Show Me How, I Can Learn to Do It: The Role of Modeling

Not too long ago, Doug decided that he wanted to learn to ski. Given that he lived in San Diego, he had never skied before but was interested in this winter sport. He enrolled in a class at the local community college in preparation for a trip to Breckenridge. During the first class session, the participants watched a video of skiers and were provided with a short reading about the dangers of skiing. During the next class meeting, the ski instructor had the class suit up despite the fact that it was 70 degrees outside. In their ski suits, with poles and boots, the class members climbed a set of stairs. When they reached the top, they saw a ski slope of sorts. This slope was mechanical and had a piece of carpet that moved. The class was told that this experience would prepare them for the downhill feel of skiing. Faithfully, Doug got onto the contraption and "skied" down the hill. To any observer, it looked more like a controlled fall rather than skiing.

For the next several sessions, the class members took time attempting to make it to the bottom of the hill without falling. They were provided lectures about various types of equipment and good-versus-bad places to ski. The teacher gave a number of quizzes, covering such topics as types of lifts, snow conditions, danger signs, and the like. One day, the class was asked to write a response comparing cross-country skiing with downhill skiing.

Doug learned a lot about skiing, but not how to ski. No one showed him the moves required to navigate the snow. No one modeled the ways in which skiers made decisions about traversing a mountainside. No one explained the split-second decisions that skiers make while skiing. And no one provided an authentic environment for learning these concepts.

The results were predictable. Doug felt like he could ski. He had done very well on the quizzes and had passed the downhill performance test. He left for Breckenridge very pleased with his progress. Unfortunately, Doug was not ready to ski based on his experiences. He fell a lot and ended up in the hospital with frostbite and injured hands. Sadly, he never skied again.

Looking back on this experience, it's easy to identify the problem. Doug lacked a model of what good skiers do. It wasn't that Doug wasn't motivated or knowledgeable. He needed to get inside the mind of an expert, someone who could explain the moves and the reasons for those moves. He needed an opportunity to think like a skier before receiving feedback and coaching about skiing.

Regardless of the learning goal, our experience suggests that novices need models to be successful. We'll focus on reading as our learning goal in this book, but we know that modeling facilitates all kinds of learning. As you read the following example from Diane's teaching, consider how instructional modeling, if played out widely, would solve many of the problems that occur for many of us on a daily basis.

From Skiing to Writing: Why Modeling Is Important

Recently, as a formative way to measure the effectiveness of her instruction, Diane asked her 11th-grade students what they thought had helped to strengthen them as writers since the beginning of the school year. While they offered many insights, the most notable was what Mario said, "You give us examples. You show us how you write it. Then you help us until we can write our own. When you teach us like this, it's easy to learn how to do it."

What Mario referred to was that, like many teachers, Diane thinks through anchor texts as examples of how to read and write the type of text the class is discussing. Some of these she writes herself and others are published works. To Diane and her colleagues, sharing a piece of text means thinking it through with the students—yes, inviting students to peek inside the instructors' minds to see what they are thinking as they read or write the text.

For example, if she addresses the California English language arts standard (California State Board of Education, 2007) that requires students to be able to "structure ideas and arguments in a sustained, persuasive, and sophisticated way and to support them with precise and relevant examples" (Writing Strategies 1.3), she shares advertisements, letters to the editor, and editorials while thinking out loud about the elements that constitute a persuasive piece of writing. By sharing these anchor texts as well as modeling how to think through the text construction, students acquire a mental graphic of a persuasive text. As Diane says, "I see that all of these begin with an introductory hook, or what we call a grabber, that captures the attention of the reader and causes us to want to read further. After the hook, the writer provides the reader with supported facts that promote his or her stance and then follow this with a statement of conclusion that moves the reader to action." This mental model supports their comprehending and writing of additional persuasive pieces.

Once they have the visual model of the format and the language of a persuasive text, students coconstruct an oral piece of persuasion. For example, they talk through a letter to the school principal about why the school should not have soda vending machines. As they craft the content, students also discuss the format. By making the first draft an oral draft, students have an opportunity to try on the academic language and instantiate in their minds the elements of structure of the targeted piece. As they coconstruct this piece, Diane supportively models as needed. For example, she might think aloud that because the audience is the principal, who likes research, it is important for them to include some data that supports their position.

Next, they are ready to transfer this new knowledge as they write a persuasive letter to a friend or a company about another topic of personal significance, such as the ill effects of unhealthy eating or why companies should not profile one type of appearance when hiring employees. This segment also begins orally as they share their ideas with a partner who offers them feedback about the content and the format. Now they are ready to independently write this persuasive piece.

Supportive modeling of this type introduces the target concepts and authentically acquaints students with academic and topical language as well as genre structure. Additionally, it helps them to acquire the security and competence they need to be successful at the task when they try it independently. Modeling provides students with pictorial, process, and linguistic examples, which serve as the cognitive hooks on which they can hang new information. As they become fluent or familiar with these dimensions, they are cognitively free to refocus their attention on expanding and transferring the informational base to new situations.

We had an affirmation that this type of instruction was really working when it was time for students to take the high school exit exam, a state requirement in California. To our surprise and good fortune, the writing prompt asked the students to write a letter to a company persuading them about something students felt was important. Although the students believed that we had known what the prompt was going to be, we were as surprised as they. Our students did very well as a result of the modeling they experienced—a 99% pass rate.

The student who didn't pass scored poorly on language conventions but fared well on content and structure. He was a speaker of African American vernacular English, and we believe that his content was superior to his ability to express that understanding with standard English. We are well aware that "it may sometimes seem that there are only two kinds of English in the United States, good English and bad English" (Hymes, 1981, p. v) and that a less-than-positive profile exists about those who do not speak what is believed to be the good English (Bernstein, 1970). This profile promulgates a deficit image of the speaker and the speaker's language that, when played out in schools and professional situations that require the good English, propels the profiled speaker in a downward trajectory of failure.

It is this realization that caused Diane to again model for this particular student how she makes a match between the audience and the way she expresses a message. For example, she used a number of photos for potential audiences (such as people at a lecture, people in Balboa Park, friends having coffee, two people talking at a bus stop) and thought aloud about how she might adjust her register for each situation. While looking at the Balboa Park picture, she said, "I see that this is a group of friends walking through our park. They're probably going to a museum. While they're walking, I bet they're talking in an informal register. If I were to join this group, I know that I could use some slang and lots of pronouns." Exposure through modeling provides a way to let this student in on the thinking process about how to construct a message for a particular audience. This type of modeling is not done to the student; rather, it is done as a shared partnership designed to offer exposure regarding language registers.

This modeling of language was a way to support this student's growing knowledge about language variations as different but not deficit so as not to disparage his home community. This is important because Edwards (2007) implored educators to expose their students to all of the language registers they will need to succeed in situations outside of their homes. Again, modeling supports this possibility.

An Instructional Perspective on Modeling

Modeling is a primary way through which teachers can offer instructional demonstrations for their students, such as showing how competent readers make sense of texts (e.g., Taylor & Pearson, 2002). Shared reading, a common form of modeling text processing, has evolved from a focus on Big Books—originally developed by Holdaway (1979, 1983) as a way for teachers to model while young students watched—to a variety of classroom interactions in which the teacher and students share a text. Currently, shared reading is a generic term many teachers use to describe a range of classroom activities, including echo reading (students repeating the words aloud after the teacher reads), choral reading (students reading aloud while the teacher reads aloud), or Cloze reading (the teacher reads aloud, pausing periodically for students to fill in the missing word) (e.g., Blachowicz & Ogle, 2001).

In their study of effective teachers in England, Topping and Ferguson (2005) noted, "Effective teachers were more likely to teach a range of literacy skills and knowledge at the word, sentence and text level through the context of a shared text" (p. 126). According to the study, shared reading involved the teacher modeling reading by focusing on word- or sentence-level work. Alternatively, Short, Kane, and Peeling (2000) described shared reading as allowing the teacher to "model and support the use of cues and self-monitoring reading strategies, which may include the use of pictures to help construct meaning, making predictions, rereading, segmenting and blending phonemes, and finding familiar word chunks to decode words" (p. 287). As can be seen in these two definitions, specifically identifying what constitutes a shared reading is difficult; however, both definitions indicate that shared readings have potential with older readers and should not be limited to use with emergent readers.

Regardless of the definition, modeling is a key component of reading instruction. Consider the personal perspective of Dr. Jill Bolte Taylor, a Harvard neuroscientist who suffered a major stroke at age 37; her mind deteriorated enough that she could not walk, talk, read, write, or recall anything of her previous life. Over several years and with a significant amount of work and the support of her mother, Taylor regained most of her skills. In her book, *My Stroke of Insight: A Brain Scientist's Personal Journey* (2006), Taylor discussed the difficulty in learning to read again and how the modeling and guidance provided by her mother were critical in her rehabilitation. In the excerpt below, we get a rare glimpse into the reading development process from someone who was a very skilled reader and had to relearn everything, from letter recognition to comprehension:

> Learning to read again was by far the hardest thing I had to do. I
> don't know if those cells in my brain had died or what, but I had no

recollection that reading was something I had ever done before, and I thought that the concept was ridiculous. Reading was such an abstract idea that I couldn't believe anyone had ever thought of it, much less put forth the effort to figure out how to do it. Although G.G. [her mother] was a kind taskmaster, she was insistent about my learning and placed a book titled *The Puppy Who Wanted a Boy* in my hands. Together we embarked upon the most arduous task I could imagine: teaching me to make sense of the written word. It befuddled me how she could think these squiggles were significant. I remember her showing me an "S" and saying, "This is an 'S,'" and I would say, "No Mama, that's a squiggle." And she would say, "This squiggle is an 'S' and it sounds like 'SSSSS'." I thought the woman had lost her mind. A squiggle was just a squiggle and it made no sound.

My brain remained in pain over the task of learning to read for quite some time. I had a real problem concentrating on something that complicated. Thinking literally was hard enough for my brain at this early stage, but jumping to something abstract was beyond me. Learning to read took a long time and a lot of coaxing. First, I had to understand that every squiggle had a name, and that every squiggle had an associated sound. Then, combinations of squiggles—er—letters, fit together to represent special combinations of sounds (sh, th, sq, etc.). When we string all of those combinations of sounds together, they make a single sound (word) that has a meaning attached to it! Geez! Have you ever stopped to think about how many little tasks your brain is performing this instant just so you can read this book? (p. 101)

Taylor's experience with learning how to read again mirrors the struggle so many students face as they seek to wrestle with every little squiggle. As well, her mother's efforts to teach her daughter resonates with our own experiences as teachers—"the kind taskmaster." Shared reading, modeling thinking while reading, is part of a larger instructional plan first described by Pearson and Gallagher (1983). The gradual release of responsibility model of instruction suggests that the teacher first models then guides students toward independence. The idea is that, over time, the responsibility (cognitive load) shifts from the teacher doing all or most of the work to students doing significant amounts of work. Our adaptation (Fisher & Frey, 2008a) of this model contains four components: (1) focus lessons, (2) guided instruction, (3) productive group work, and (4) independent learning.

For us, one significant key to learning is the focus lesson in which modeling first occurs. As was evident in the instruction Diane shared with her 11th-grade students, it is during the initial focus lesson when the teacher establishes a purpose and models his or her thinking. This is the time when students in Diane's English class get to see writing modeled through authentic writing examples that are shared, discussed, and analyzed by someone who has the expertise to let the students in on how to make sense of this new information.

This needs to happen all day long for students. During science instruction, students should get to see scientific thinking being modeled, and during history class, students should observe historical thinking by their teachers who have expertise with this information. This modeling needs to occur so that students realize through conversation with their teachers the specifics of the new information they are learning. This is when a clear purpose as well as the process for learning is established.

After the focus lesson, students experience guided instruction and group work that is also designed to support and empower the development of the knowledge they need to move toward independence. When this happens, students are being taught in ways that are supported by brain and learning research (Willis, 2008). For example, think about Diane's students who were

- Engaged and making connections among their personal language experiences and interests and the new information
- Processing the modeled information while constructing the new knowledge
- Investing in writing tasks they were helping to create
- Intrinsically motivated because they wanted to share their message
- Solving authentic problems related to their everyday school life
- Challenged yet unthreatened because they were well supported by their teacher
- Employing more than one modality (visual, auditory, kinesthetic)
- Making decisions while engaged in interest-driven investigations which supported the development of their new knowledge

Let's think about this as we move into the next chapter, where we can step back just a bit to relate what we already know about a gradual release of responsibility model of instruction and shared reading.

Looking Ahead

In the next chapter, we augment this information about effective instruction by exploring what is known about what happens in the brain as one reads. These insights support the importance of instructional modeling. From there, we explore the ways in which teachers use modeling to develop students' thinking about text. More specifically, we consider the ways in which teachers model comprehension, word solving, text structures, and text features.

In each of the subsequent chapters, we integrate theories of cognitive science and neuroscience with best practices in teaching. We do so for science, social studies, mathematics, English, and elective classes. Along the way, you meet a number of teachers who use modeling to facilitate their students' understanding of complex ideas. The teachers and students exemplified in this book are composites of our own work as well as teachers and students we have observed (Fisher, Frey, & Lapp, 2008); the voices are authentic, although the names are not.

The final chapter introduces you to a number of real teachers who use modeling to improve student learning. These teachers are featured on the DVD that is included in this book.

CHAPTER 2

Why History, the Brain, and Teachers Support Modeling

We were reminded of the importance of instructional modeling when a student in our graduate thesis-writing class told us she had been worried that we would ask her to write a thesis without ever having seen one. She was quite relieved when we entered the classroom carrying many bound theses, which we asked the students to survey as we talked them through the process of thinking about writing and then how to write a thesis. As we thought aloud about the process, we related it to our classroom instruction and the research questions that arise for us on a daily basis. We then asked these graduate students to identify some of their classroom wonderings. As they relaxed, they shared questions like the following:

1. Do children transfer knowledge about how to write (e.g., thinking about audience, tone, revising) across contexts more thoroughly when writing is taught as part of content mastery rather than as part of a prescribed writing time?

2. How do teachers differentiate assignments within cooperative groups during reading/language arts?

By looking through these concrete models while listening to us think aloud about how we initiate research questions and then design, execute, and evaluate a research study, we offered our students one pattern or model of how to engage in this process. These graduate students were able to use our way of thinking as researchers as an archetype as they initially mimicked and eventually constructed their own pictorial, linguistic, and procedural models of how to conduct a study that would support their thesis writing. They did this as they talked and shared ideas with us and their peers. In this way, their inner speech (or **articulatory loops**) had an opportunity to try on the new language.

As they engaged in this new learning activity, their minds were growing another neuronal network. This happens to each of us every time we learn or engage in a new activity because, when we hear, see, or think about something novel, a new group of **neurons** is linked together in a fresh way in our brains. The more we practice this new information, the more familiar the information in the **neuronal pathway** becomes and the less difficulty we have with retrieval and related learning.

This is why it's so important to provide time for students to practice any new learning that you're modeling. Without this practice and use, the brain will prune this information, which it views as irrelevant. It will do so to make space for the next new learning to occur. This is why you sometimes remember something for a short time, probably for a test, but you are no longer able to retrieve it later. It was pruned because of lack of use. Any information that is worth knowing must be practiced and used often if we want to retain it. Think about this neuronal pathway like any other trail you've explored: The more you travel it, the more familiar and permanent all dimensions of it become.

Isn't it logical then that as teachers engage in instructional modeling students are provided with the organizational pattern, picture, or structure they need to make sense of the topical information and

language being shared? You can realize why this is so effective now that you understand how one's brain searches for patterns or carves out pathways to make sense of incoming information (Fabbro, 2001).

More specifically, in the case of our graduate students, our modeling provided them with the supports they needed to be able to engage in secure and rich dialogue, which resulted in their being able to connect the physical and conceptual information related to thesis writing. The actual theses provided the realia, or authentic examples, to be perused as we explained and thought through several studies. We knew our modeling had been effective when multiple students nodded in agreement as one said, "I'm getting the picture. I have an idea for a study I'd like to do." We then knew that they had grasped the concept and were having the opportunity to own the language and the practices associated with conducting research.

Are you thinking that this sounds like it takes a lot of time? Are you wondering how to rearrange your schedule and get everything taught? If you answered yes to these questions, think about what's happening inside your head. You're experiencing some instructional disequilibrium because this isn't familiar information to you. Your brain hasn't seen this scenario of instructional modeling as a possibility. You've been focusing on teaching through a different lens. Stick with us as we share some additional information that we hope will help you to construct a new neuronal pathway. To address the question of time, we've found that modeling throughout our instruction is just a rearrangement of the instructional time; we spend a greater amount of time up front with the thinking aloud explanation and conversation rather than later reteaching when students don't understand because they failed to develop a clear picture or "envisionment" of the process, language, or task.

To even better understand the importance of modeling as an instructional approach, let's consider modeling by addressing the following questions:

1. Is modeling something new? What's its history?
2. How does modeling relate to thinking? What's the neurological basis?
3. Should modeling be a significant dimension of instruction? If so, how would this look in the classroom?

A Historical Perspective on Modeling

Have you ever wondered how the early primates or hominids had so many successes without formal language systems? They learned to mimic one another. When one figured something out, others watched and tried it. They relied on this ability to locate the best food sources, avoid dangerous areas, and adopt innovations that improved the likelihood that they would survive another day. Indeed, our species is known for its social nature; those that were not inclined to life within a group were at a distinct disadvantage because they had fewer opportunities to mimic and thus learn from one another.

Neuropsychologist Merlin Donald (1991) proposed that the transition from hominid to human can be described through three distinct cognitive advances: mimicry, language development, and external storage of information (chances are you are initiating another neuronal network as you read this). The evolution of a nonverbal "mimetic culture" started a period of startling growth as early humans began to congregate, communicate, and cohabitate. Even more important, this growing proclivity to mimic the actions of others led to vocal mimicry, the earliest stage of the evolution of spoken language.

With the accompanying biological changes that allowed early humans to speak (the larynx dropped lower in the throat), it appears that human language, which emerged in Africa about 50,000 years ago, had many of the grammatical and lexical structures associated with modern languages (Diamond, 2006). This theory of a "protolanguage" as an ancestor to modern day language remains a controversial one. Scientists, linguists, and anthropologists have differing opinions about the extent to which culture and biology interacted with humans' ability to move from vocal mimicry to language.

However, there is agreement that early language moved from pidgin (with a simple structure and few words, used as communication among people with no shared system) to a creole (a language with more formal syntactic, morphological, and phonological rules that emerges when communication systems meet). What is most fascinating is that the evolution from pidgin to creole often appears to take place within a generation, meaning that it is the *children* who invariably push the language (Calvin & Bickerton, 2000). You've probably experienced this as you've listened to the conversations of your children or students as they invented new ways to say the simplest things. As soon as they think an adult is trying to learn the new jargon, the words change. This isn't something unique to this generation; you can perhaps remember creating language with your own "homies."

Returning to Donald's (1991) theory of three major cognitive advances of the species, the final development occurred when humans figured out that they could store information outside of their own bodies. Think for a moment of the possibilities this offers and all of the advancements that have since occurred. One no longer had to vocally share where the best hunting could be found; it could be represented in figures that held meaning for others, even those not present initially. Wolf (2007) described the empowerment of this realization as two human "epiphanies...*symbolic representation* and... the insight that *a system of symbols can be used to communicate across time and space*" (pp. 25–26, emphasis added). This—the notion that marks, tallies, or shapes could preserve information and that this information could be understood long after the maker was gone—changed civilization.

The first writing systems, called token systems, were mostly for accounting purposes—they were used to record crops, cattle, and the like. But it is the use of these token writing systems that resulted in the brain reestablishing the way it works: The brain needed to establish new neuronal pathways to link the "visual areas [in the **occipital lobe**] to both the language and conceptual systems located in the **temporal** (two front sides) and **parietal** (middle) **lobes** and also to the visual and auditory specialization regions called '**association areas**'" of the brain

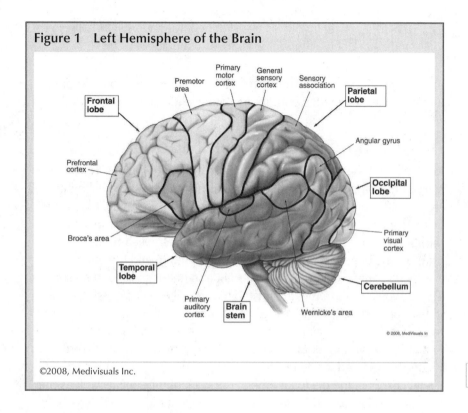

Figure 1   Left Hemisphere of the Brain

Primary
motor
cortex

Premotor
area

General
sensory
cortex

Sensory
association

**Parietal
lobe**

**Frontal
lobe**

Angular gyrus

Prefrontal
cortex

**Occipital
lobe**

Broca's area

Primary
visual
cortex

**Temporal
lobe**

Cerebellum

Primary
auditory
cortex

**Brain
stem**

Wernicke's area

© 2008, MediVisuals In

©2008, Medivisuals Inc.

(Wolf, 2007, p. 29). Figure 1 shows a diagram of the left hemisphere of the brain with several of these areas identified.

Before long, increasingly symbolic and formalized writing systems emerged across the world. And eventually, educational systems were established to teach the young how to read and record information using these systems. As a result, these neuronal pathways were further developed through the social practices of mimicry, oral language, and writing. You can see why modeling can be considered a bedrock of teaching. Now, let's draw from the insights of our ancestors as we create a pattern of modeling as a tool for learning. In particular, we believe the following:

- The first stage of modeling involves mimicry: "Watch me as I do it."

- The second stage involves oral language as teachers and students collaborate: "Let's do it together."

• The third stage involves transforming information externally so that independence occurs: "Let's talk or write about it."

In the next section, we further explore what is known about the brain and how this knowledge contributes to our understanding of modeling.

A Neural Perspective on Modeling

Regardless of the subject we teach, we're all brain workers. Teachers spend their days trying to influence what is stored in students' brains. It's really quite simple: There are a limited number of inputs that the brain accepts and a limited number of outputs that the brain can produce. Inputs come in the form of sight, hearing, taste, smell, and touch. Outputs include such modes as speaking, writing, and moving.

In teaching, we tend to rely on sight and hearing for good reason. These two senses are directly related to the language processing centers in the human brain. While there is evidence that humans are hardwired to listen and speak, reading and writing are not natural processes. Reading and writing require the use of biological systems that were originally designed for other functions. Reading requires activation of the **visual cortex** in the occipital lobe at the back of the skull as well as the listening center located in the temporal lobe (refer again to Figure 1). For a fascinating look at the process of reading in the human brain, see *Proust and the Squid: The Story and Science of the Reading Brain* (Wolf, 2007).

Of course, both working memory and long-term memory are involved in reading. There are a number of brain structures involved in creating memories, and one of significance is your **hippocampus**. Picture a sea horse with curved ridges of tissue. This is how your two hippocampi look inside your temporal lobes, which are on both sides of your brain. The hippocampus helps you to store and retrieve your memories. For our purposes here, we'll focus on the ways in which modeling can help get information into and then used by the brain.

There are a few key ideas about the human brain that should influence every teacher, the first of which is that *experience changes neural connections*. When we experience something, neurons fire. In 1949, Hebb suggested that neurons that fire together simultaneously are more likely to fire together in the future. According to Hebb's theory, these networks are created and established through experiences. Siegel (2000) rephrased Hebb's theory and simply stated, "Neurons that fire together, survive together and wire together" (cited in Wolfe, 2001, p.

76). And here is the key to instruction: Teachers have to help neurons fire and then provide continued experiences so that these neurons wire together.

The second key idea, which we have alluded to already, is that *there is no reading gene*. This means that each and every brain of each and every student in your class must be taught to read. Reading isn't something, like hair or eye color, that is transmitted from one generation to the next. Reading is a complex, rule-based system that must be imposed on biological structures that were designed or evolved for other reasons. Yes, most children are born with the right structures, but these structures don't inherently know how to read. Children must be taught how to read, and we believe this should begin early and through the most authentic and natural language-based ways.

Teaching the brain to read across multiple genres requires that specific behaviors need to become so automatic that they work without being given conscious attention. Building on the 1974 work of LaBerge and Samuels, Bloom (1986) explained **automaticity** as the brain developing its ability to "perform a skill unconsciously with speed and accuracy while consciously carrying on other brain functions" (cited in Wolfe, 2001, p. 102). This is why developing automaticity with decoding and word recognition is so essential to comprehension. Automaticity allows the reader to focus attention to the meaning rather than the process for acquiring the meaning.

As Squire and Kandel (2000) demonstrated, three areas of the brain are involved in the early stages of learning a new skill or procedure: the **prefrontal cortex**, which serves as the storage area for information that needs to be housed for a short-term; the parietal lobe, which serves to bind visual features; and the **cerebellum**, which plays a major role in sensory perception. These three areas allow the learner to pay attention, execute the correct movements, and sequence the steps. Think about how important early and natural practice becomes in eliminating ambiguities among the object features of letters in words. As the task or procedure is learned and becomes automatic, these three areas of the brain become less involved, and the **sensory-motor cortex** seems to become more engaged. In other words, more cognitive space is devoted to learning a new skill than executing a learned skill. The reader can thus refocus attention to comprehending the meaning of the associated words rather than to identifying a target letter or word. Taken together, these two ideas suggest that teachers must provide students with experiences and that these experiences must be repeated often enough until they are internalized as habits (automaticity).

Unfortunately, teaching isn't this easy, which brings us to the third key idea. *The brain prefers novel stimulus* and pays less attention to familiar information. For example, when driving we pay attention to the new route or the voice speaking on our GPS rather than the familiar routines of the act of driving. So when we safely arrive at our new destination, we feel a sense of accomplishment or satisfaction. The **midbrain**, deep inside the cerebrum, is generally responsible for regulating motivation and reward processing. This area responds better to novelty than to the familiar, which helps explain why rote memorization of reading facts doesn't seem to work. Simply said, when the input becomes increasingly familiar, we pay less attention to the information. In fact, we often aren't sure if we unplugged the coffee pot or closed the garage door because we do these things without attending to them. As we gain proficiency as readers, we do not read letter by letter or focus our attention on the letters because through supported practice the process becomes automatic.

But there is another side to this, which brings us to the fourth key idea about modeling and the brain: O*ur brain is hardwired to mimic and imitate.* Most of us have learned about motor neurons and sensory neurons. The former cause movement and take information away from the central nervous system (CNS) while the latter carry information to the CNS. But recently researchers have identified a new type of neuron, the **mirror neuron**. These unique cells are active when we do something *or* when we watch someone do something. They seem to mirror the behaviors regardless of whether or not we're the one moving!

Can you see how important this information is to your role as a modeler of information when your students are learning something new? Exactly. Their neurons are firing as they watch you perform or think through the unfamiliar information. So the way that we model for students certainly affects how they are influenced to perform and execute human features from imitation to empathy to language learning and use (Hurley, 2008). This might just be one of the most important and under-reported findings for educators this decade. (For an interesting account of the discovery of mirror neurons, see Lea Winerman's article published in *Monitor on Psychology* [2005].)

Modeling, then, is important from both a historical and neural perspective. As we have seen, our species has successfully used modeling to survive. Modeling also has a neural basis in that our brains are wired to mimic what they're exposed to, especially when information is novel. In addition, there is an instructional rationale for modeling, which we will explore next.

An Instructional Perspective on Modeling

Returning to our previous topic of the brain, we know that priming helps our brain pay attention and learn. What this means is that there is evidence that humans can alert their brains to pay attention for specific stimuli. For example, we can look for a specific type of food when we go to the store or search a bookshelf for a specific book. This is why it's a good idea to state the purpose of the lesson or identify a goal before modeling. As Wolfe (2001) noted, letting students in on the objective of the lesson "allows the brain to anticipate the critical features of ideas and increases the likelihood that the brain will focus on the essential information" (p. 34).

Once the purpose has been established, the teacher can model his or her thinking. The remainder of this book provides additional examples of teacher modeling of reading. The topics for this book come from an observational study of 25 teachers who each modeled their own thinking in four ways (Fisher, Frey, & Lapp, 2008). From the most to least common, this group of teachers modeled comprehension, word solving, text structures, and text features. Each of these areas frames a full chapter with examples from various content areas. Table 1 provides a summary of these topics—to prime your brain for this information.

Of course, modeling is only part of the instructional cycle. In addition to the focus lesson, students need to see visual representations as a part of guided instruction. This is the time when teachers use pictures, diagrams, and replicas, as well as prompts, cues, and questions to facilitate the transfer of responsibility to students. Guided instruction can occur in a whole-class setting but is much more effective when done with small groups of students that are intentionally selected. Small-group guided instruction is particularly advantageous for fostering oral language as students begin to apply what is being modeled: using the academic vocabulary of the content.

For example, following a shared reading that included many visuals about the human eye and vision in which Ms. Cody modeled her thinking, students in the biology class read a primary source document about visual fields in groups of four. As they did so, Ms. Cody met with these small groups to guide their understanding. With one of the groups, she had the following conversation:

Ms. Cody: See the illustration here and how the eyes are seeing two objects, a truck and a key?

Andrew: Yes, the person would see both things, right?

Table 1 Shared Reading Components

Component	Definition	Subtypes
Comprehension	Strategic and active moves to understand the text	Activating background, inferring, summarizing, predicting, clarifying, questioning, visualizing, monitoring, synthesizing, evaluating, and connecting
Vocabulary	Focus on solving an unknown word, not providing the definition of the word	Inside the word strategies (word parts such as prefix, suffix, root, base, cognates, and word families) Outside the word strategies (context clues) Use of resources (peers, dictionaries, Internet)
Text Structures	Structures used in presenting information that readers can use to predict the flow of information	Compare/contrast, problem/solution, cause/effect, chronological/sequence, descriptive story grammar (plot, setting, character, conflict, etc.)
Text Features	Components of the text added to increase understanding or interest	Headings, captions, illustrations, bold or italic words, charts, tables, diagrams, glossary, index, or graphs

Ms. Cody: Yes, but how? That's the question with visual fields. Let's look at the left eye on the temporal side. What is that registering?

Melissa: The image of the truck is traveling to the same side of the brain, to the occipital lobe.

Ms. Cody: Yes, perfect! Now do that for all four areas on the diagram.

The key to guided instruction is not telling students a second or third time the information they've already heard nor is it doing the work for them. Instead, teachers have to be strategic about the statements they make and the questions they ask.

Our instructional model also includes time for productive group work. This occurs while the teacher is not present with a group of students. In Ms. Cody's biology class, students used reciprocal teaching to read and discuss the text (e.g., Palincsar & Brown, 1984). Again, as with guided instruction, this is another opportunity for students to use oral language to strengthen their newly constructed associations or neuronal pathways. Reciprocal teaching enjoys such a strong research base as an effective means of comprehension instruction (e.g., Rosenshine & Meister, 1994) because the areas of focus—summarizing, question generating, clarifying, and predicting—are so powerful. However, we believe the role of student modeling in reciprocal teaching has been obscured. Stated simply, this instructional arrangement allows students to try on modeling for themselves. The following is an exchange between students as they jointly read a text titled "How the Brain Sees" from an online article from BBC News:

Melissa: I'll start by summarizing. This article was about how the brain sees, not the eyes. But the cool thing is that the scientists who did this work figured out the brain can see things unconsciously, even when the person can't see it visibly.

Tien: I better go next, 'cause I gotta clarify. If I've got this right, they showed people lines...vertical and horizontal lines. It says some of the lines were invisible. The first time I read it, I totally didn't get it. But then I reread this part [points to paper] and there's a point at which "the space of the lines becomes too fine" and it starts to blur. That made me jump back down to here [points to a paragraph lower on the page] where the author said that the scientists showed lines that couldn't....

Leo: The lines couldn't be seen by the naked eye....

Tien: Yeah, yeah, and the brain still acted like it could see the lines.

Leo: Blurred! So I'll go ahead and ask a question I used in my own head. I checked out the heading that said "Conscious Knowledge" and turned it into a question: What is conscious knowledge?

Sarah: Good question, and like, it doesn't really say here. You have to infer, you know, read between the lines. It says, "Your visual cortex isn't telling you everything."

Leo: I did the same thing. I used it as a reminder that conscious means what you're aware of.

Sarah: Ok, so I'll do my job. I'll predict. Since this was a pretty short reading and we finished it, I'll make a prediction about Ms. Cody. I predict this info is going to show up on a test!

The biology students used reciprocal teaching as a means to jointly understand complex texts and to model for one another how they comprehend. As you observe your own students engage in reciprocal teaching, notice the subtle mimicry that occurs as they begin to take on each other's language patterns. As with our socially oriented ancestors, mimicry and oral language offer pathways to learning new ideas.

The fourth aspect of our instructional model is independent learning, the time when students get to formalize their knowledge especially through writing. You'll recall from earlier in the chapter Donald's (1991) description of the third major cognitive advance— external storage of information. Independent learning is an ideal time for students to record their thinking through essays, summaries, graphic organizers, and the like. As with other skills, we hope that there is plenty of teacher modeling that occurs prior to independent writing. Consider, for example, Sarah's summary of her learning, shown in Figure 2. She wasn't simply assigned a reading and asked to write a summary alone. She had time during guided instruction when Ms. Cody fostered verbal summaries of the information about diagrams of the brain. In addition, students discussed their understanding of an article during productive group work. Sarah was well equipped to write the summary.

Ms. Cody's lesson, like the others presented in this book, illustrates instruction within environmental settings that engage students in active learning involving multiple dimensions of their brains. This type of involvement is essential for students to develop and retain learning. Medina (2008) offered support for active learning in his discussion of 12 scientifically based brain rules (see Figure 3) that when applied to education have the potential to offer pathways for change. For example, when he spoke about brain rules 4 (attention) and 6 (long-term memory), he reminded us that it's possible to process more elaborate information and store it for longer periods of time when one's attention has been piqued by an emotional connection with the content of the material.

Sound familiar? Of course, because teachers seeing this type of engagement and active learning occurring for their students are thrilled,

Figure 2 Sarah's Summary of Visual Fields in the Brain

The visual fields of the brain are more complex than you might think. For one thing, the eye doesn't really see. It only takes in the images, but it is the brain that does the seeing. That's because the brain has to interpret the images. If the optic nerve is damaged, it will mean blindness because the image cannot travel to the occipital lobe. But if the occipital lobe at the back of the brain is damaged, a person can still "see" but can't understand what is being seen.

There is more evidence for this. Scientists did experiments showing line patterns right on a person's retina. The lines were too close together for a person to see clearly and they would be blurry. But then they did another experiment. They showed lines that were too fine to be seen by the eye. The brain of the person still acted like it saw the lines, even though the lines were too tiny to see. The brains of the people acted like it was blurry. So the brain sees, not the eye.

Figure 3 The Brain Rules

🏃 **EXERCISE | Rule #1:** Exercise boosts brain power.

❌ **SURVIVAL | Rule #2:** The human brain evolved, too.

🔄 **WIRING | Rule #3:** Every brain is wired differently.

❗ **ATTENTION | Rule #4:** We don't pay attention to boring things.

🕐 **SHORT-TERM MEMORY | Rule #5:** Repeat to remember.

📅 **LONG-TERM MEMORY | Rule #6:** Remember to repeat.

🛏 **SLEEP | Rule #7:** Sleep well, think well.

💥 **STRESS | Rule #8:** Stressed brains don't learn the same way.

🔥 **SENSORY INTEGRATION | Rule #9:** Stimulate more of the senses.

👁 **VISION | Rule #10:** Vision trumps all other senses.

🚻 **GENDER | Rule #11:** Male and female brains are different.

🔍 **EXPLORATION | Rule #12:** We are powerful and natural explorers.

Note. From Medina, J. (2008). *Brain rules: 12 principles for surviving and thriving at work, home, and school.* Seattle: Pear Press. Copyright © 2008 by J. Medina. Reprinted with permission.

and they strive to create this type of instructional encounter daily. While the goal is clear to all of us, the "how to" of involving students in active learning every day and every period is often the focus of our educational conversations. Medina's book *Brain Rules* (2008), which presents easy-to-read chapters titled after each of the rules—exercise, survival, wiring, attention, short-term memory, long-term memory, sleep, stress, sensory integration, vision, gender, and exploration—is very appropriate for collaborative book club conversations among colleagues. The ensuing conversations will offer insights about how to create active learning among engaged learners.

Keep This in Mind

To help you remember this information, we've included a song about brain vocabulary in Figure 4. In addition, if you watch the first video clip on the DVD included in this book, you'll see a group of students singing this song. We hope the song and the students signing it will help you process the information. Like so much of what we learn, knowledge about modeling is a synthesis of many fields. The field of history informs our understanding of the roles of mimicry, oral language, and external storage of information in learning. As well, the wealth of information available on the brain continues to push our thinking, in many cases confirming what we in the reading field have known for years. This is especially true when it comes to our understanding that there is no reading gene, that experience changes thinking, and that novelty stimulates learning. Finally, our understanding of modeling as a cornerstone of instructional effectiveness has been confirmed countless times in research studies and in our classroom experiences. A gradual release of responsibility model that shifts the cognitive load to the learner through increasingly self-regulated activities builds knowledge. Call it neuronal networks or schema-building or just good teaching. The historical, neurological, and educational fields point to the same advice—let me show you, then you can make it your own.

Figure 4   Brain Song by Linda Lungren

(Tune: Down by the Riverside)

Gonna learn all about the brain
The parts and what they do.
Thinking and vision too.
Feelings and how you move.

Gonna learn all about the brain
The parts and what they do.
Learn all about the brain.

The lobes are sections of the brain:
Temporal helps you hear,
Occipital interprets sight,
Parietal sees it all.

Now don't forget the frontal lobe,
It's always full of thought.
Frontal, Temporal,
Occipital, Parietal Lobes.

The cortex is the outer part
And helps in many ways
Visual cortex controls our sight
Prefrontal cortex our memory.

Association cortex syncs them up.
Vision and hearing.
The cortex is the brain's outer part.

Without the cerebellum you would fall.
Coordination is the key
The cerebellum does for me
Plus balance on a beam.

The hippocampus banks for me
All of my memories.
Learn all about the brain.

When we learn something new,
Neuronal pathways form.
And when we do it again,
Neuronal pathways grow.

Automaticity occurs
Your life is now a breeze.
You move without having to think.

CHAPTER 3

Comprehension: Building on Background, Motivation, and Knowledge to Increase Understanding

C *omprehension* is an elusive term, and one that has generated a great deal of debate in the reading world. *Webster's Collegiate Dictionary* offers this definition for *comprehension*: "capacity of the mind to perceive and understand." Accepting this definition requires an understanding of two significant ideas. Reading is about understanding meanings contained in texts. As such, comprehension requires that the reader can decode the words on the page and assign meanings to those words. That's the superficial comprehension tested through literal level questions. But true comprehending is more than making meaning from print. It's about integrating what's in the text with the reader's perceptions. And these perceptions are formed based on previous knowledge and experiences, which are often unique to individuals. Wolf (2007) offered an elegant description of the moment when a young reader begins to comprehend at a deeper level, a moment that moves from simply lifting words from the page to taking action based on reading. In her words, "emotional engagement is often the tipping point between leaping into the reading life or remaining in a childhood bog where reading is endured only as a means to other ends" (p. 132). Rosenblatt (1960), who coined transactional theory in the 1930s, described what occurs between the reader and the text in this way:

> The reader and the text are more analogous to a pianist and a musical score. But the instrument the reader plays upon is—himself. His keyboard is the range of his own past experiences with life and literature, his own present concerns, anxieties, and aspirations. Under the stimulus and guidance of the text, the reader seeks to strike the appropriate keys, to bring

the relevant responses into consciousness. Out of the particular sensations, images, feelings, and ideas which have become linked for him with verbal symbols, he creates a new organization. This is for him the poem, or play, or story. (pp. 304–305)

Years ago, Thorndike (1971) suggested that reading with comprehension is

a very complex procedure, involving the weighing of each of many elements in a sentence, their organization in the proper relations to one another, the selection of certain connotations and the rejection of others, and the cooperation of many forces to produce the final response. (p. 323)

These forces are many and include decoding, fluency, vocabulary, attention, motivation, memory, and knowledge.

Let's work at comprehending a six-word story written by Ernest Hemingway. He wrote the following work of fiction to win a bet, and some say it's the best thing he ever wrote:

For sale: baby shoes, never worn.

The words are easy enough to understand. The "hardest" word is two syllables and five letters long. But ask yourself about what it took to understand this story. In Thorndike's (1971) words, what forces did you use? Naturally you had to decode the words and assign meaning to them. Simply using those forces would not result in the deep understanding Hemingway intended nor would it allow for the transaction with text Rosenblatt (1960) discussed. What background knowledge was required? What inferences did you make? How did the punctuation help you understand the author's meaning? And what of the emotional engagement Wolf (2007) described? Because you comprehended at a deep level, you were able to fill in a whole backstory on what had occurred. You related to the pain of the parents at the loss of their newborn and would probably have read the next sentence, if one existed, because in six short words you were caught up in the hinted tragedy.

Do we want any less for our students? And yet so often we entice them to the doorway of comprehension, only to block their efforts with texts that are too difficult.

A Caution About Hard Books

Consider the reading you do most often. You probably find it easy, and it should be. Most of what we read should be effortless. Really, who perpetuated the falsehood that if the reading is easy, it's not worthwhile? Readers gain new information, consider alternative perspectives, and extend their thinking while reading things that they *can* read. Remember the Hemingway short story? The reading was easy, but the ideas contained in it were complex, compelling, and profound. Reading should not be a laborious process in which the reader struggles through a text, word by word, trying to figure out what is happening. When that occurs, readers are banished to the "childhood bog" Wolf described (2007, p. 132).

Hard books are difficult in a number of ways. Commonly hard books contain a lot of vocabulary that is unknown to the reader. There is more about vocabulary in the next chapter, but for now keep in mind that word choice is one way to make reading more or less difficult. Hard books also tend to have longer, complex sentences in which ideas are embedded. In these cases, the reader must be able to parse the sentence to get to the ideas. But that's not to say that simply leveling books by text complexity is the answer. Both interest and motivation have a profound effect on the difficulty the reader experiences. For instance, books about life science that some people might find hard don't create problems for Nancy. She's highly interested in this topic and is motivated to read and learn more. This motivation and interest, combined with her experience with the subject, make these books more accessible than might be expected. Giving these same books to a reader with limited background or prior knowledge on the subject and no interest or motivation will not result in understanding. And more important, the reader can't simply try a bunch of strategies to make sense of the text. Strategies, like the ones we will focus on in this chapter, are useful when the text becomes somewhat difficult and the reader wants to understand. These strategies do not work for incomprehensible texts that the reader does not care to read. And at the risk of exploding a classroom myth, assigning difficult texts and then trying to compensate with comprehension strategy instruction simply doesn't work (Fisher & Frey, 2008c).

What then is the role of modeling comprehension if we cannot force students to understand texts in which they aren't interested and for which they don't have the background and prior knowledge? Our experience has been that it is helpful for students to have labels for the types of strategies used by good readers when the text becomes more difficult. The goal is to teach for metacognition—the conscious decision making that a reader uses to regain meaning when the comprehension process bogs down. In terms of brain function, this is the **frontal lobe** kicking in to action to make some executive decisions about what should be done. In the reading research field, this is self-regulated learning modeled on the research around effective readers (Paris, Wasik, & Turner, 1991; Pressley, 2002b).

Before we consider the ways in which teachers model their comprehension, we need to consider a number of factors that have an impact on understanding, including the role of background and prior knowledge, the role of motivation, and the role of hierarchical knowledge. Understanding these three ideas will ensure that we model comprehension strategies that students can use with texts they encounter in and out of the classroom.

The Roles of Background and Prior Knowledge in Comprehension

As readers, we're always activating our knowledge base and comparing it with what we are reading. In other words, we compare what we already know with what we are reading. This is what most people think of as engaged reading, and what Rosenblatt (1960) meant when she used the analogy of the pianist and the musical score. Developmental psychologist Jean Piaget argued that we do this with all kinds of learning, not just reading. Piaget (1970) believed that humans organize information into a schema—a mental representation of related perceptions, ideas, or actions—and that these schemas are the building blocks of thinking. As we see in the next section, schemas remain the basic idea of knowledge organization. Piaget also believed that knowledge expands by reformulation of what is already understood and that this reformulation occurs in three ways: assimilation, accommodation, and equilibration.

First, assimilation increases knowledge by integrating information into existing schemas. If you have, for example, a schema for birds that includes flying, feathers, and egg-laying, you can assimilate hens, eagles, doves, and the like into your knowledge base. Second, accommodation increases knowledge by modifying schemas to account for new experience. Returning to the schema for birds, when confronted with an ostrich or penguin, you'll have to modify your understanding to account for this new information, that not all birds can fly. And finally, equilibration changes knowledge by creating a coherent balance between schemas and sensory evidence. Once again returning to the schema for birds, when confronted with creatures from the past, you'll use both assimilation and accommodation to determine which were birds. Through equilibration, Piaget (1970) suggested that humans attempt to maintain a logical internal mental structure that allows us to make sense of the world. When this internal structure is challenged, humans attempt to assimilate and accommodate information to achieve balance again. For Piaget, disequilibration provided a great learning opportunity. Psychologists refer to it as cognitive dissonance—that unsettling feeling that two ideas don't connect. Teachers capitalize on this when they use anticipation guides to alert students to what they know and don't know or when they use a dramatic demonstration of a principle to prime students for a learning experience.

However, Piaget (1970) left out an important element—the ways we learn from one another. (You'll recall in Chapter 2 that we described mimicry as a learning tool.) In response to Piaget's neglect of social interaction, Vygotsky (1986) suggested that advanced concepts (schema) appear first in social interactions. Whereas Piaget emphasized schema development within the individual, Vygotsky argued that these concepts gradually become accessible to an individual through interactions with others. For example, the possibility of riding a bike wouldn't occur to a child unless she had seen others riding one first. She then builds a schema around movement, wheeled vehicles, and fun. To explain this phenomenon, Vygotsky introduced the zone of proximal development (ZPD), which he suggested is the difference between what a child can do independently and the capabilities of the child when interacting with others.

From these two theorists, a couple implications arise. First, students need lots of experiences. These experiences allow for both assimilation and accommodation, and even periodically require equilibration. Second, students need guidance to continue learning. There are specific teacher actions that work in the ZPD, scaffolding what a student can do. The experiences we provide for students must be planned to build their competence. In providing these classroom experiences, we have to think about what our students already know. Thus, learning is about modifying what is already known and not simply pouring facts into the learner's mind. We think of this knowledge in two ways: background and prior knowledge. Both are critical for comprehension:

- *Prior knowledge* includes information that was, or should have been, formally taught before the current lesson. This includes previous school years as well as previous instructional units. For example, students in high school U.S. history should have already learned about the American Revolution, Declaration of Independence, and Civil War. In an algebra class graphing linear equations, students should already be familiar with factoring and solving linear equations.

• *Background knowledge* includes the information a person has because of lived experience. Accordingly, background knowledge may vary considerably between two students. One may have extensive experience with the sea whereas the other may have only seen ocean pictures. Background knowledge is influenced by both direct and indirect experience (reading or talking).

Let's take a minute to explore the ways in which a teacher might incorporate the use of background knowledge during modeling. Ms. Madrigal, an art teacher, displayed *The Red Book* (Lehman, 2004) using a document camera and data projector. As she examined each of the wordless pages, she shared her thinking with students. When looking at the cover, she said, "It seems to me that this boy is cold. I see his hat, scarf, jacket, and boots. But it's just all red on the cover so I don't have all of the clues I need to make a good inference or prediction. But I can tell that he's walking quickly and when I add that to the clothing, I predict that it's cold where he is." As she talked about each page, she described her thinking. Several pages into the book, she said, "Oh, wow, now that's a surprise. The boy on the island is looking through the book to the girl in the cold city and vice versa. I'm wondering if they'll ever get to meet or if it will be like other books where the reader gets to meet people through books that you'll never really meet in person. I remember meeting Charlotte from *Charlotte's Web* [White, 1952] and I'll never forget her advice. Have you met someone in a book that you'll never forget? Let's take a minute and talk with a partner about who we've met in books."

Obviously Ms. Madrigal modeled more than background and prior knowledge, but the importance of this information in understanding this wordless book cannot be understated. In making inferences about the cold, Ms. Madrigal drew on her background knowledge. In predicting, she also drew on her experience with the world. And further, when she made a connection between the wordless book and a popular children's book, she drew on her prior knowledge.

The challenge related to background knowledge is that we can't directly teach it. There are, however, effective ways for developing this type of knowledge. Most important, students need to read a great deal to build their knowledge. Reading widely influences a student's background knowledge and level of vocabulary (Marzano, 2004). In addition to wide reading, students need direct experiences, which can occur through field trips, hands-on experiments, guest speakers, projects, internships, and other experiential learning events.

While critical for comprehension, background and prior knowledge are not enough to ensure success. As we know from Nancy's reading of life science, motivation also plays a factor in comprehension.

The Role of Motivation in Comprehension

The research on motivation in learning is rich. Reading researchers Guthrie and Wigfield (2000) wrote extensively on the importance of tapping into the motivation of learners. They defined it as "the individual's personal goals, values, and beliefs with regard to the topics, processes, and outcomes reading" (p. 405). They made a point of distinguishing this from attitude, which is related to the degree that one enjoys a task, and interest, which is specifically related to the nature of the topic. For instance, Doug has a good attitude about reading because he finds it relaxing, while Diane reads nearly anything about her favorite city, Paris, because she is interested in it.

Guthrie and Wigfield (2000) conceived of motivation as the extent to which reading a particular text aligns with the learner's goals. If the text appears to fulfill a purpose, such as completing a project, motivation is likely to go up. Motivation is intrinsic as well, such as when a person reads something because it satisfies a curiosity. The number of hours many of us spend on the Internet is likely related to this intrinsic motivation. How often have you launched a search for a particular topic, only to find yourself visiting a half a dozen other websites because your attention turned to related information? Motivation is associated with self-efficacy, the sense that one is sufficiently challenged yet not overwhelmed by the difficulty of the task. We need only look at the number of university extension courses and Internet-based seminars to see that many adult learners seek experiences that expand and challenge their thinking, yet are not so difficult that they will feel defeated by the content.

Of course, motivation is of interest to teachers because it is directly related to learning. There is supporting neuroscience evidence to suggest a biological basis for motivation and its link to memory formation. For example, research evidence suggests that people are more likely to remember and recall when their brain perceives a reward. Research on rewards also suggests that the **mesolimbic pathway** of the brain (associated with emotion) and the hippocampus (affiliated with learning) work in concert with one another. In particular, these two regions work together to alert the **neocortex** to prepare itself for learning (Adcock, Thangavel, Whitfield-Gabrieli, Knutson, & Gabrieli, 2006). While this study used extrinsic rewards, it raises questions about perception of reward, even those that are internally induced, and its relationship to learning. An analysis of the 1996 National Assesment of Educational Progress national achievement scores established a correlational relationship between engagement and levels of text comprehension, noting that students who reported higher levels of engagement with the text passages scored higher (Campbell, Voekl, & Donahue, 1997).

So what does reading motivation look like in the classroom? Guthrie and Wigfield (2000) gave several recommendations about that. In particular, they noted that the need for interesting texts that have a real-world application. They also recommended that students are provided a range of choices in what will be read. The teacher's use of encouragement and praise is important, especially when those interactions provide informative feedback. Students also benefit from evaluation opportunities that provide feedback on their progress toward goals, especially those that have a student-centered focus, such as portfolios, projects, and peer response sessions. And as Vygotsky (1986) noted, the social aspect of learning cannot be overlooked, especially when small groups of students are engaged in meaningful reading activities that serve a larger purpose.

Eleventh-grade U.S. history teacher Mr. Reynolds takes all this into account when he designs units of study. He introduced his students to a unit on the Japanese internment camps of World War II through a series of photographs of artifacts from the era, including a button announcing "Jap Hunting Season" that began to appear soon after the attack on Pearl Harbor. He led a choral read aloud as partners stood to read a series of headlines that appeared in the *Los Angeles Times*, including ones that announced "Suicide Reveals Spy Ring Here" (December 19, 1941) and "[Governor] Olsen Says War May Hit State" (January 26, 1942). He then conducted a shared reading of an editorial (Takaki, 2000) that originally appeared on February 2, 1942, which stated the following:

> Perhaps the most difficult and delicate question that confronts our powers that be is the handling—the safe and proper treatment—of our American-born Japanese, our Japanese-American citizens by the accident of birth. But who are Japanese nevertheless. A viper is nonetheless a viper wherever the egg is hatched. (p. 145)

By this point in the lesson, his students began to understand the hysteria and racial hatred brewing on the U.S. west coast in the weeks and months following Pearl Harbor. He shows them one more artifact—Executive Order 9066, signed by Franklin Roosevelt, ordering all Japanese and Japanese Americans be removed immediately to internment camps scattered across a dozen states. He modeled his thinking as he reads the following sentence:

> I hereby further authorize and direct the Secretary of War and the said Military Commanders to take such other steps as he or the appropriate Military Commander may deem advisable to enforce compliance with the restrictions applicable to each military area herein above authorized to be designated, including the use of Federal troops and other Federal Agencies, with authority to accept assistance of state and local agencies. (Executive Order 9066, 1942, ¶4)

"Whoa, I think I know what this means. I got a chill as I read it, but I'm going to reread it to see if I'm right," explained Mr. Reynolds. He reread the sentence more slowly, then said, "It's a lot of legalese, but there are a few phrases here that help me to understand that President Roosevelt was making it clear that military force would be used, if necessary. I'm chunking some important phrases in my mind: *Secretary of War, Military Commanders, take such other steps,* and *enforce compliance with the restrictions.*" He underlined as he went. "I'm inferring the meaning of these phrases. Roosevelt is making it very clear that military force will be used against Americans. I can see that he chose his words carefully—especially when he says, 'enforce compliance' in the same breath with 'War' and 'Military.' I'm beginning to understand that this message was meant to intimidate the Japanese and Japanese Americans into doing what they were told, to not resist against the Army."

Mr. Reynolds had taken his understanding of motivation to heart as he chose compelling texts to engage his students and build a purpose for reading further. Soon after, his students worked in groups of five to analyze artifacts and other primary-source documents he had selected in thematic units titled Removal, Life in the Camps, Military Service of Japanese Americans, and Seeking Justice. He also focused some of his instructional time on one more element necessary to increase motivation—strategy instruction. As Guthrie et al. (1996) reported, students who demonstrate growth in reading motivation also exhibit an increase in their use of strategies during reading. It is likely that is related to their sense of competence and a feeling that they have control over their learning.

The Role of Hierarchical Knowledge in Comprehension

Consider what happens when you think about a concept or word, for instance *dog*. You rapidly begin sorting through your vast knowledge base, recognizing that a dog is a domesticated mammal with four legs and fur. You consider the features of a dog—the wet nose, wagging tail, and friendly disposition. Perhaps you cataloge the types of dogs you know: Chihuahua, golden retriever, collie, and poodle. Your experience plays a role, too, as you recall childhood pets or memories of a nasty bite. Perhaps you are reminded of dogs in literature, from White Fang to Lassie. If you drew a hierarchical map of what you knew, a portion of it might look like the one shown in Figure 5.

Your ability to be able to interpret and retrieve information is due in part to your brain's organizational structure. As knowledge is acquired, our brain arranges it in a hierarchical structure. Even more remarkable, it is constantly rearranged as new information is added. Now think about the beauty of this elegant hierarchical arrangement. Other ordering systems wouldn't work well; for example, an alphabetical or chronological structure would leave us endlessly looking for *dog* because we would have to either rifle through all the *A*, *B*, and *C* concepts first, or we would have to calendar each time we were exposed to a dog. Imagine how long it would take to complete a test!

Teachers have long known and understood this and have applied the principles of hierarchical knowledge to instruction. In particular, we use maps similar to the one seen in Figure 5, although the focus is more likely to be on literary devices or binomials or ancient Rome rather than dogs. There is evidence that **hierarchical representations** of knowledge are very useful for learners with little background knowledge because it gives them an external structure where one does not currently exist internally (Potelle & Rouet, 2003). However, the basic principle of hierarchical representations remains the same—we organize information efficiently based on formal knowledge and prior experience, with the larger concepts at the top and threads of increasing detail arranged beneath those larger concepts. It is that organization that allows us to retrieve information and to figure out where to plug in the new learning (Kintsch, 1988).

Consider the average 13-year-old's closet, and you get the idea of what can go wrong when we don't teach for hierarchical representations. Left to his own devices, he will probably just keep throwing clothes, shoes, sports equipment, and the ephemera of adolescence into a growing mound in the closet and then quickly shut

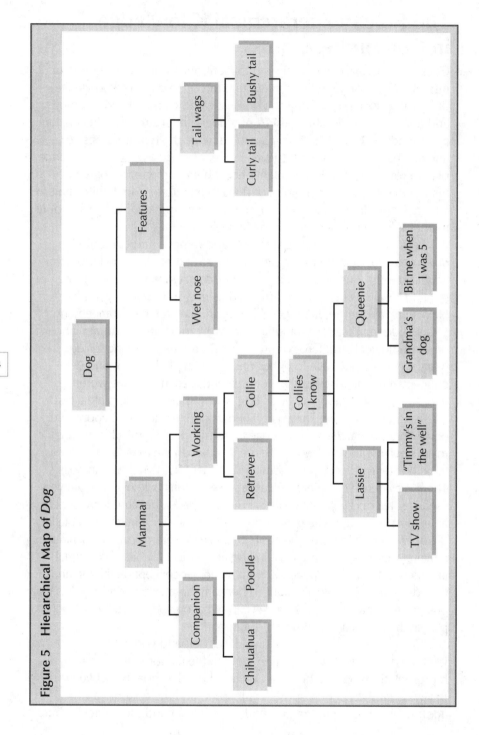

Figure 5 Hierarchical Map of *Dog*

the door so it doesn't spill out. When asked to find his soccer shoes so the family can leave for the game, he makes a half-hearted effort to root through the clutter and then declares that someone has taken them. In fact, the shoes are in there, but he can't find them because there isn't an organizational structure. If he had (and used) a basket for shoes, or if he kept all his soccer equipment in a sports bag, then he would be able to find his cleats right away. Even more important, he would know where to put a new pair of shoes or a new set of shin protectors. Notice, too, that there is conceivably more than one way to organize his closet. A basket of shoes is one way; a sports equipment bag is another.

This ability to arrange information in a hierarchical structure resides in the neocortex (Latin for "new bark"), the thin outer layer of the brain. Hierarchical arrangements of information abound in our world and occur across space and time (e.g., the human body, the floors of a building, words in a text) (Hawkins & Blakeslee, 2004). Not only do those hierarchical representations allow us to retrieve information, but they also help us learn new information. And this may be the place where we get it wrong (or at least only half right) when it comes to teaching the new information—we tend to move conceptually from top to bottom (larger concept to detail) when in fact it is the movement from bottom to top that seems to yield new understandings. It's that lower level "stuff" that lets us learn through a process called **temporal pooling** (Hawkins & Blakeslee, 2004). This pooling of separate pieces of information is analyzed for commonalities and moves up the chain—a movement "from many to one" that allows the learner to understand the bigger conceptual frameworks that organize many otherwise disparate ideas. Look at Figure 5 again, but this time read it from bottom to top. The phrase "all roads lead to Rome" comes to mind, as the information is pooled into increasingly larger chunks of information. Now consider the analogy of the 13-year-old's closet as he puts away his soccer shoes. The ability to develop an organizational system begins with understanding the individual pieces. In truth, the development of a hierarchical structure requires that cognition occurs in *both* directions— from concept to detail, and from detail to concept.

Another name for this is *inductive* and *deductive reasoning,* and it has everything to do with how we model our comprehension of text. When we model how we understand, as we predict, as we make connections, and so on, we also need to show students how we chunk details together to form a larger concept (inductive reasoning). As well, we must show them when we recognize a major concept and assign a detail to it (deductive reasoning).

Goals for Comprehension Modeling

So far we have made the case, both from the fields of reading and neuroscience, about the role background knowledge, motivation, and hierarchical knowledge play in comprehension. In the next section, we explore in more detail the types of strategies teachers model for their students. But before we go on, we must pause to discuss the goals of comprehension modeling.

Our first caution is that comprehension strategies don't become the curriculum. Too often we have watched well-intentioned teachers bludgeon the life out of a strategy in an attempt to teach it—six weeks of predicting, followed by three weeks of visualizing, then nine weeks of inferring (because that's harder, they argue). It is essential to remember how these strategies are used in real reading, not the school version. Effective readers draw upon strategies *as they are needed* and *when they are needed.* They let the text and their own degree of understanding dictate when they must fall back on a strategy to make sense. Modeling the use of reading comprehension strategies should be no less authentic. Effective readers don't pause to make a prediction at the beginning of every text, no matter what. They make a prediction when it is needed and when the text signals them to do so. For instance, a rousing whodunit demands that the reader predict and revise her predictions as new clues become available. However, an Agatha Christie fan doesn't need to pause at the cover to make a prediction about what the book will be about because she already knows what to expect—she has read 10 of them already. When we model reading comprehension for our students, we let the text tell us what to do, and we apply more than one strategy across a piece of text.

Which brings us to our second goal of comprehension strategy instruction—developing skilled readers. We agree with the definition Afflerbach, Pearson, and Paris (2008) crafted in an attempt to clarify the ways in which the field discusses strategies and skills:

> Reading strategies are *deliberate, goal-directed attempts to control and modify* the reader's efforts to decode text, understand words, and construct meanings of text whereas *reading skills* are *automatic actions* that result in decoding and comprehension with speed, efficiency, and fluency, usually without awareness of the components or control involved. (p. 368, emphasis added)

More important, the authors' definition of strategies and skills has important ramifications for instruction. The ultimate goal of strategy instruction is that over time these strategies become skills—an "automatic action"—that frees up the brain's **working memory** to formulate sophisticated understandings of what is read. As Afflerbach and his colleagues (2008) noted, "In this view of learning, deliberate reading strategies often become fluent reading skills" (p. 368). Our focus should be on developing habits that move readers to higher levels of automaticity in comprehending text (Frey, Fisher, & Berkin, 2009).

We worry that an emphasis on the mechanics of implementing a strategy can get in the way of a reader who is becoming more skilled. For example, we have seen this happen with literature circle conversations that become stilted because the teacher insists on clinging to the assigned role sheets when they are no longer needed (Daniels, 2006).

In modeling and teaching for reading comprehension, it is important that the tail is not allowed to wag the dog. Strategies should be taught well and taught for metacognitive awareness so that when the going gets tough, an effective reader knows how to fall back on strategies to make sense of difficult text. For instance, many of us will write notes in the margins of a difficult reading because we know from experience that it helps us clarify our understanding. But we don't write marginalia in everything we read, because we are understanding just fine and to stop to write a note would slow us down. The goal over time, therefore, needs to be focused on building habits of reading comprehension and not stopping short at the level of strategies.

Modeling Comprehension

In the examples that follow, we highlight a specific comprehension strategy that readers use while reading. It is important to note that the teachers highlighted in this section did not focus on a single comprehension strategy for the entire text. Instead, they allow the text to guide them in determining what to model for students. A list of the most common comprehension strategies that are modeled by teachers is included in Table 2. In Appendix A, we provide a sample of the comprehension modeling a teacher did based on the book *Wolf Rider* by Avi (1986). As you can see in Appendix A, teachers do not focus on modeling one strategy at a time, but rather allow the text to guide their thinking, and thus what they model.

Establishing Purpose

As Marzano, Pickering, and Pollock (2001) noted, establishing a meaningful purpose is a prerequisite to effective learning. From the standpoint of neuroscience, establishing the purpose at the beginning

Table 2 Comprehension Strategies That Can Be Modeled

Strategy	Definition
Establishing Purpose	Identifying and understanding why something is being read
Inferring	"Reading between the lines" to understand implied information
Summarizing and Synthesizing	Identifying the major points and ideas from a selection
Predicting	Using available information to make an educated guess about what might happen next
Questioning	Maintaining an inquiry focus before, during, and after reading
Visualizing	Creating a mental image of the text in your mind
Monitoring	Noticing when comprehension is lost and applying strategies to regain meaning
Determining Importance	Finding main ideas and separating them from details
Connecting	Relating the text to personal experiences, other readings, and the world

of an event primes the brain for future learning (Wolfe, 2001). The same is true for reading. Readers have to understand why they are reading each specific text that they read. Stated another way, readers need clear, appropriate, and specific goals prior to reading (Pressley, 2002b). Of course, readers do this naturally as they read things they have chosen to read. Consider the difference in purpose you have for reading a newspaper and reading a novel. As a skilled reader, you understand that your purpose can change based on the type of reading, the genre of the text being read, and what you might do with the information after reading. In general, readers establish some of the following purposes:

- To be informed about the biological, physical, or social world
- To follow directions
- To be entertained
- To find out how to do something

To help students understand and establish purpose, teachers need to model the questions that readers ask themselves, such as (a) Why am I reading this? (b) What am I trying to learn? (c) What is the information about? and (d) What type of text is this? Establishing purpose is, at least in part, a way to help students pay attention to what they are reading.

For example, when looking at a website about the carbon cycle (see earthobservatory.nasa.gov/Library/CarbonCycle), ninth-grade earth science teacher Ms. Herrell explained her reason for looking at the specific page. "I'm looking for something specific. I know that I have to remember a lot of information about the carbon cycle, so I want to see if NASA provides a good visual that I can use to remember. I don't need to read all of the text on this page to find out if there are some good visuals here. My purpose is to discover visuals that I can use to study." She quickly modeled her purpose and proceeded to skim and scan the pages to determine if the text was a good match for her need.

Alternatively, a middle school English teacher informed his class that he "wanted a little entertainment before getting down to the business of writing. I looked for a poem that would make me smile because I know that I have some serious work to do soon. So, I found an Ogden Nash poem about a germ. I want to read this, just to make me smile and remember why I work so hard in teaching writing. Listen as I read [reads poem]."

A mighty creature is the germ,
Though smaller than the pachyderm.
His customary dwelling place
Is deep within the human race.
His childish pride he often pleases
By giving people strange diseases.
Do you, my poppet, feel infirm?
You probably contain a germ.

(Copyright © 1933 by Ogden Nash, renewed.
Reprinted with permission of Curtis, Brown, Ltd.)

Both teachers understood why they had selected their respective texts and were able to communicate that with their students. In doing so, they ensured that their students knew what to pay attention to and what was expected of them after the reading.

Inferring

Understanding implied messages is critical for comprehension. Authors do not state everything explicitly and instead rely on the reader to supply information and draw conclusions based on what is known. Inferences occur "when the reader activates information that is evoked by, yet goes beyond, the information that is provided explicitly in the text" (van den Broek, Fletcher, & Risden, 1993, p. 170). Sometimes referred to as "reading between the lines" or a blending of "text-based connections and schema-based connections" (Herber, 1978, p. 154), inferring is a complex cognitive process that can easily go astray. As McMackin and Witherell (2005) noted, "Lack of sufficient background knowledge, 'inconsiderate texts' [Armbruster, 1984], weak vocabulary knowledge, lack of relevant experiences, and many other factors contribute to the level of difficulty readers encounter when making inferences" (p. 246).

There are two types of inferences as described by educational psychology researchers McKoon and Ratcliff (1992)—minimal and elaborative. The first type, minimal inferences, occurs almost naturally and is readily available to the reader. For instance, in the sentence "Vultures flew overhead as the exhausted cowboy collapsed beneath the blazing desert sun," the minimal inference is that the birds were in the sky. In addition, we know it is hot, based on the description of the sun. As such, these are not the types of inferences that typically need to be modeled. However, the more elaborative inferences include the recognition that vultures wheeling the sky are often awaiting the death of a creature, and that in this case it might be that cowboy. Other elaborative inferences fill out the scenario. We visualize a scene from a movie western, perhaps imagining the cowboy struggling on his hands and knees. Those elaborative inferences are more complex and require explicit modeling. Recall the discussion on hierarchical knowledge and the pathways that move both up and down the map. Kintsch's (1988) assertion that learners spent part of their time pooling details into larger representations is borne out in this example. We gather up chains of associated information and use the ones that fit best to fill in what is missing.

Graphic novels are especially useful in modeling elaborative inferences. The space between the panels is called the gutter, and it is the place where the reader must make inferences (McCloud, 1994). Consider the use of a single page from Will Eisner's book *New York: The Big City* (2000) (see Figure 6). Your understanding of this page is based on your ability to infer. Do you think that the two people are in an argument in the first few panels? If so, how do you know? Nancy likes to imagine (infer) that the man is apologizing in panel 5. So then, did you infer that they made up? Interestingly, from the worm's eye view, you can make a number of inferences about what's happening on the street. This is what readers have to do all of the time. Modeling inferring,

Figure 6   Worm's Eye View Graphic Novel

41

especially with highly visual sequential art, can help students build this habit and apply it to increasingly complex pieces of text.

Summarizing and Synthesizing

Readers cannot remember everything that they read; the cognitive load is simply too heavy. Instead, readers have to remember salient points and key ideas. The word *summarize*, according to the Webster's dictionary, means to

- Present the substance or general idea in brief form
- Create a concise, condensed account of the original
- Cover the main points

Summarizing improves students' reading comprehension of fiction and nonfiction alike as it helps the reader construct an *overall* understanding of a text (Rinehart, Stahl, & Erickson, 1986). When summarizing, students focus on the gist of the reading, not the trivia or details; Table 3 contains a number of clues that help readers develop quality summaries. Summaries can be oral or written but must be shorter than the original and must not appropriate the authors' words (Frey, Fisher, & Hernandez, 2003). There are two kinds of summarizing that students are asked to do:

1. Summarizing and synthesizing significant ideas in a single text
2. Summarizing or synthesizing significant ideas across texts and drawing conclusions based on the information in more than one text

Table 3   Clues to Use When Summarizing a Text

- Specifics from the title
- Information at the beginning of the selection
- Questions that the author asks or implies
- Surprises or revelations
- Information presented in tables or figures
- Details that are repeated
- Headings, subheads, and italicized text
- Changes in character, tone, mood, setting, plot
- Data provided at the end of the selection

As can be seen in these tasks, summarizing is related to synthesizing, which Keene and Zimmermann (1997) defined as

> the process of ordering, recalling, retelling, and recreating into a coherent whole the information with which our minds are bombarded every day. It is the uniquely human trait that permits us to sift through a myriad of details and focus on those pieces we need to know and remember. (p. 169)

Summarizing and synthesizing are complimentary but slightly independent. Synthesizing allows the reader to add information to the summary—it's the integration of information and not only a retelling.

Ms. Jenkins modeled summarizing and synthesizing after reading a text selection about genetic variation. The text contained lots of details and was very interesting. The margin notes contained bits of information that captured the readers' interest. As Ms. Jenkins noted after reading aloud the text and modeling along the way, "Wow, that's a lot to remember! I'm going to take a minute right now and summarize what I remember. The notes on the side of the text about eye color were exceptionally interesting. Do you remember that? Talk with a partner about the ways in which eye color is carried from one generation to the next."

The students in this biology class quickly turned to one another and began talking. Nicole said to Josiah, "The grandparents had different colored eyes; one blue and one brown. But the brown ones are dominant, so all of their children had brown eyes, but had the recessive gene for blue eyes." The conversation continued for a few minutes until Ms. Jenkins began speaking again.

"Yes, inherited eye color is very interesting, but it's not the main point of the selection. I know that the author was trying to provide me with an example, but I need to remember the major points. One major point that I'd like to summarize is that genes contain the instructions needed in order to construct a human body and that variation in the code produces individual differences. Can you summarize another major point with a partner? Then we'll collect the major points and create our synthesis." Her summary provided students with an example of the type of thinking required of the task. She also invited students into the process as they discussed major points with a partner. Using her example, students identified key ideas from the reading, and the resulting summary included the main ideas. Along the way, students gained a valuable experience—they learned how to summarize and were not told to simply summarize.

Predicting

Making an educated guess about what might happen next, given the available information, is known as predicting. Humans have been predicting since time immemorial. The ability to predict has been tied directly to the survival of the species (Wolsey & Fisher, 2008). When making predictions, readers typically use the following processes: (a) activating prior knowledge, (b) thinking on both literal and inferential levels, (c) supplementing or modifying their knowledge base, (d) linking efferent and affective thinking processes, (e) making connections, and (f) filling the gaps in the author's writing (Block, Rodgers, & Johnson, 2004). In other words, predicting requires the use of a number of skills and strategies.

Children understand the importance of making predictions. For example, McNay and Melville (1993) demonstrated that elementary school children understood predicting as "an internal process in which one uses knowledge to anticipate a future event" (p. 561). The challenge is to help students understand that predicting is not just a wild guess, but rather a hypothesis formed from using the available information.

Equally important is the notion of learning from predictions, especially predictions that are incorrect. Some of the common clues readers use to make predictions include word choice, tone or mood, literary devices (flashback, foreshadowing, symbolism), and text features such as headings, subheadings, and highlighted terms. Modeling the use of predicting should include revisiting missed clues that cause inaccurate predictions. Students shouldn't leave the predicting experience saying to themselves, "Oh, I guess I was wrong; it's just a guess anyway."

During his modeling of a text about the Civil War, Mr. Sotelo used the title of the article to make his first prediction. He said, "The title gives me a great clue about the reading. It says 'It Could Have Been Called the Boys' War.' Given that I know we're studying the Civil War, I can use the available information to predict that the war identified in the title is the Civil War. I can also predict that there must have been a number of children in this war, given that the author is saying that we might consider a different name for this war. I'll return to this prediction at the end of the reading." In this case, Mr. Sotelo used predicting to also establish a purpose.

Mr. Jessop, modeling his thinking using predicting, focused on the use of literary devices during a reading of Edgar Allan Poe's short story, "The Fall of the House of Usher." In his words, "I always look for foreshadowing as a way to predict what's going to happen. I know enough about foreshadowing to know that this is cool technique for keeping the reader's attention. It's like when you watch a horror movie, and you know something creepy is going to happen before the character does. And Poe sure writes creepy! I read this sentence describing Roderick Usher's house on page 41. 'I looked upon the scene before me—upon the mere house, and the simple landscape features of the domain—upon the bleak walls—upon the vacant, eye-like windows— upon the few rank sedges—and upon a few white trunks of decayed trees....' Man, I got that creepy feeling. His eyes are all darting around. I think that's why he used all those hyphens between phrases, so I'd get that jumpy feeling. That's when I knew he wasn't just taking some time to describe the house. He was warning me that the house was going to be like the people in it. These words, like *bleak, vacant, rank, decayed*— that's a heck of a way to describe a very troubled family."

As with Mr. Sotelo in the previous example, Mr. Jessop didn't confine his modeling to prediction only. The text dictated that some visualizing was happening as well, and the English teacher didn't concern himself with only modeling a "pure" form of prediction. As Mr. Jessop said, "Poe writes to overwhelm our senses, so why wouldn't I share that with my students? He wants to make our minds race, and I want my students to see how my head is spinning."

Questioning

As readers, we regularly generate questions before, during, and after our reading. These questions may focus on the text's content, structure, or language. The evidence base for questioning is filled with effective ways for readers to question. For example, students can be taught to ask questions of the author (Beck, McKeown, Hamilton, & Kucan, 1997). Alternatively, Raphael and Au (2005) demonstrated the impact that teaching students questioning skills has on comprehension and test taking. In their research, readers were taught to focus on four types of questions:

1. *Right there.* The answer to this type of question can be found on a specific line of text.
2. *Think and search.* The answer to this type of question can be found in the reading, but not in a specific place in the text. Instead, the reader must compile information from several places.

3. *Author and you.* The answer to this type of question cannot be found in the text. Instead, the reader must draw inferences based on the reading.

4. *On your own.* The answer to this type of question may not require reading of the selection. Instead, it draws heavily on the personal experiences and opinions of the reader.

Regardless of the approach, it is important that students learn to *ask* questions and not simply to answer questions posed by the teacher. Responding to questions asked by the teacher does not build students' habits nor does it facilitate deeper understanding of texts. Durkin (1979) demonstrated this is her seminal research on comprehension instruction in American classrooms when she found that the majority of questions asked by the teacher were for assessing comprehension, not supporting it, as evidenced by the fact that questions were rarely posed before or during the reading.

To model questioning, Mr. Coltero read aloud a text from *Discover Magazine* about Phineas Gage, the man who survived a penetrating brain injury in 1858 (this case is a classic in neurology textbooks). After reading about the injury in which a railroad tamping rod traveled through Phineas's skull, Mr. Coltero posed two questions to his students, "I have two questions at this point in the text. First, how did Phineas Gage survive the penetrating brain injury? And second, for how much longer will he live? Turn to a partner and ask a question about the text. Don't answer my question; instead ask your own."

In doing this, Mr. Coltero modeled the importance of questioning, showed the use of academic language related to questioning, and provided his students an opportunity to engage in the process of question formation. Herein lies the power of modeling: Students can use the example provided by their teacher to generate ideas and apply the strategy. Some of the questions the students asked included the following:

- Did he get an infection?
- Has this ever happened before to anyone else?
- When did he die and how?
- Where was his brain damaged and how did he change?
- Why didn't they take Phineas to a hospital?

Ms. Ocampo uses Bloom's (1986) taxonomy to demonstrate her questioning skills. She has posters of each type of question (knowledge, comprehension, application, analysis, synthesis, and evaluation) and models asking herself questions as she reads. In doing so, she names the type of question and then provides students an opportunity to create other types of questions on their own. For example, after reading a primary source document "The Act of Supremacy" in which King Henry VIII of England is declared head of the Church in England, Ms. Ocampo said, "Let me see if I have this right. I have a knowledge question, Who is this about? It really is about King Henry VIII. I also have an analysis question, Why does he want to be head of the church? Oh, then he can grant himself the divorce that he wants because the Pope won't do so. Those two questions help me think about this document. Can you write down two questions on your own, not knowledge or analysis, about this reading?"

Visualizing

Visualizing, or forming a mental image, is what writers hope their readers do with the texts they create. Writers evoke images for their readers through words. As we read, our brains create the proverbial "movie in your mind." Koch (2005) suggested that this cinematic experience is not limited to reading, but rather is how humans experience and process sensory information. Reading is visual information that activates areas of the brain that have stored other memories. We know, for example, that reading about a particular smell can evoke a strong reaction, even in the absence of the actual olfactory stimulus (think of the words *armpit*, *rose*, and *diaper*). Similarly, reading can evoke our other senses. Consider the range of senses that are evoked from a seven-word Haiku written by one of the masters, Yosa Buson, 1716–1783:

> a tethered horse
> snow
> in the stirrups

Can you feel the cold? Can you see the horse standing in the cold with snow filling the stirrups? In addition to the sensory information, does this evoke a memory or emotion?

As you considered your sensory reaction to the Haiku, did you also think about the role that background knowledge or experience had in your understanding of the text? As we have noted, background knowledge is a significant predictor of comprehension and something that we have to attend to in classrooms. Providing students with examples of visualizing helps them build background knowledge and experience the activation of that knowledge while reading.

After reading the opening paragraph for Chapter 3 of *The Outsiders* (Hinton, 1967), Ms. Taylor visualized the scene for her ninth-grade students. The chapter opens with the fact that two girls don't have a ride home and want to call their parents for a ride. The boys talk them into accepting a ride home. Ms. Taylor said, "I can just see the scene, can't you? The movie is over, it's getting late, and they need to get home or they're busted. I can see the looks on their faces. They're worried about being late and they're worried about getting in the car with Two-Bit. Show me that look on your face. [pause] Yep, there it is. You can see it too."

Ms. Meyers also used visualizations with her science students. For example, she periodically displayed a webpage with information about recent earthquakes in California (quake.usgs.gov/recenteqs) and then visualized where the quake was and how strong it was. For example, she said, "Oh, there was a quake this weekend in Tecate. I've been to Tecate and can picture the people there on the market street making salsa and tortillas. I see that the quake was only 2.0 and it happened at 4:00 PM. It only lasted a few seconds so I don't think that people really even felt much. When I see 2.0, I visualize people going about their day and most of them not even noticing that the ground shook a bit. I'd like to see the waveforms [opens the page]. These waveforms confirm my thinking. They show a fairly small event that didn't last too long." For students to try on visualizing that is more than a simple picture, they need to have examples that are complex and varied. When their teachers share the visual representations they create, student understanding is increased. But more important, when students have lots of examples of visualizing, they begin to engage in this behavior automatically, which is the goal of reading after all.

Monitoring

Comprehension monitoring is the capacity of a reader to notice while reading whether a text is making sense or not. Monitoring is a habit for effective readers; we tend to know right away when a text is not making sense. Most readers have had the experience of reading along and suddenly realizing that they have no idea what they just read. This may be because they are tired (reading too late at night in bed, for example) or because the text is simply too difficult. In addition, the reader might have encountered some of the following (e.g., Collins & Smith, 1980; McKeown & Gentilucci, 2007; Yang, 2006):

- New words or known words that do not make sense in context
- Sentences that are vague, ambiguous, or inconsistent with background knowledge

• Paragraphs in which relationships are unclear, conflicting, or connected in several possible ways

The difference between skilled and struggling readers is in what they do when comprehension is compromised. Skilled readers do not simply notice that they have lost the meaning. They also have plans for fixing up their comprehension. Wilhelm (2001) provided a flowchart that teachers can use to help students monitor their comprehension and use fix-up strategies. His flowchart can be found in Figure 7, which identifies a number of fix-up strategies.

Mr. Hargrove models monitoring for his students as a component of each reading he does. As he reads aloud, he regularly makes comments about whether or not the text makes sense. Naturally, he models a number of other comprehension strategies in each reading, too. For example, while reading the text of George Washington's farewell address (1796), Mr. Hargrove noted that the first sentence was a bit confusing. Washington's first paragraph reads,

Friends and Fellow Citizens:

The period for a new election of a citizen to administer the executive government of the United States being not far distant, and the time actually arrived when your thoughts must be employed in designating the person who is to be clothed with that important trust, it appears to me proper, especially as it may conduce to a more distinct expression of the public voice, that I should now apprise you of the resolution I have formed, to decline being considered among the number of those out of whom a choice is to be made.

Mr. Hargrove said, "I'll have to reread this as I noticed that I got a little lost in what he was saying [reads aloud the passage again]. I have to make some connections here. Washington is talking about the Presidency, but is using different language—he never actually says, 'president'. It's true that the President is a citizen who administers the executive branch of the United States government, but when he first said it that way, I wasn't sure what he was saying." Mr. Hargrove knows that this serves to remind his students about the importance of monitoring comprehension.

Determining Importance

The information that authors provide is not always of equal importance. Understanding what is important aids readers in making decisions regarding which parts of the text deserve the most attention. For

Figure 7 Flow Chart of Comprehension-Monitoring Behaviors

1 Read a passage of text.

2 Pause, ask yourself: Does this make sense? (Do this periodically; pause at ends of natural text segments like paragraphs.)
- Option, check yourself: Can I retell the important points of the last segment? Other options: Can I say it in my own words? Are my hypotheses holding up, or do I need to change my predictions?

3 If Yes, reading makes sense! Continue reading (back to #1). If No, continue to #4.

4 Ask: When did I lose track? When did it start to go wrong?

5 Isolate cause of difficulty (each difficulty is matched to an appropriate problem-solving strategy in #6). Did I:
a. Run into difficulty with a word or words? (vocabulary)
b. Stop concentrating?
c. Read it too fast?
d. Lose the thread of meaning? i.e., struggle to understand how it relates to what was written before?
e. Not know enough about the topic that's been taken up?
f. Lose image or mental representation? i.e., Can't "see" what it is I am reading about?
g. Not understand how text is organized and where it is headed, what I should expect?
h. Try a strategy that didn't work? Not know which strategy to try?

6 Use an appropriate strategy for your problem (these correspond to the letters in #5).
a. Skip the word and read to end of sentence or segment, trying to figure it out from the context. Guess the meaning or substitute a word that seems to fit and see if it makes sense.
a. Ask someone the meaning of the word, look for definition in text, look up in dictionary.
b. Reread the segment.
b. Read aloud—it can really help to hear the text. Or ask someone else to read it aloud to you.
c. Slow down and reread, or read aloud.
d. Chunk the confusing segment with what came before or what comes afterward. Try to understand a whole chunk that is short and manageable.
e. Identify the topic and bring personal knowledge to bear. What do you know about this or a similar topic that might help you?
e. Find out more about the topic—read something else that is simpler or more introductory; use a reference book; ask someone else who knows more.
f. Try to create an image or mind picture of what is going on (could use picture mapping, tableaux, or mapping techniques from next chapter).
g. Ask: How is the text organized? How should what comes before help me with my problem? (Very helpful to know that in an argument a claim is followed by evidence and evidence is usually followed by a warrant; in cause and effect text structures, causes are followed by effects; in classification, one class or category is followed by a parallel category, etc.)
g. Recognize and use text features and cues to text structure like transitions, headings, illustrations, captions, and charts, etc.
g. Ask: Am I supposed to make an inference? Fill a gap in the story? Put several pieces of information together to see a pattern?
h. Read on and see if the confusion clears up.
h. If still confused, try another strategy or ask for help. Ask a peer, then the teacher or another expert reader.

7 Check understanding—if Yes, back to #1 to continue reading; if No, ask for help.

Note. From *Improving Comprehension With Think-Aloud Strategies: Modeling What Good Readers Do* by Jeffrey Wilhelm. Copyright © 2001 by Jeffrey Wilhelm. Reprinted by permission of Scholastic Inc.

instance, some of the information is detail level and is of secondary importance. Other information provided by the author supplies background for an idea or passage. Some details are critical for deep understanding. Other strategies or skills included in this book, including inferring, visualizing, predicting, and synthesizing, require that the reader can distinguish between what is noteworthy and what is less important in a text. As Harvey and Goudvis (2000) noted, "Determining importance means picking out the most important information when you read, to highlight essential ideas, to isolate supporting details, and to read for specific information" (p. 117).

In addition to focusing attention and making certain that other comprehension skills can be used, determining importance ensures that the reader has sufficient working memory to understand the text. Readers cannot store all of the information presented in a text in their minds. Sifting through information to determine the most important points ensures that working memory is not overloaded and continues to process information. If working memory is overloaded, the reader doesn't have a clear idea about what he or she read and has a difficult time using the information presented in the text.

The ways in which readers determine what is important is based in a large part on their purpose for reading. For example, based on a question raised in class related to climate change, Mr. Bradford modeled searching through websites to find specific information. Along the way, he made notes that would help him answer the question. He noted places where information was interesting but not related to his purpose. At one point, he said, "Now that's an interesting fact. I didn't know that coral reefs are extremely sensitive to small changes in water temperature. But that's not going to help me answer the question about the causes of global warming."

Another clue readers use in determining importance relates to text features. We have included an entire chapter devoted to text features such as headings, graphs and charts, boldfaced or italicized print, summaries, quotes, and marginal notes. In terms of determining importance, these features guide readers toward big ideas and important information. They also serve to supplement texts and, as such, provide secondary information. Readers must understand the difference and attend to the main ideas. For example, while reading from a primary source document in a history text, Ms. Marcamp commented on the illustration and it's usefulness in summarizing the text. "Wow, now this really helps me know what the author thinks is important. This one graphic contains all of the information presented in the section of text thus far. That's a pretty good clue about its relative importance."

Table 4   Tips for Identifying a Topic Sentence

Type of Topic Sentence	Explanation
General	The topic sentence is usually more generic than the other sentences in the paragraph or section. In general, the topic sentence contains a number of ideas or discusses several things. Plurals and the words many, numerous, or several often signal a topic sentence.
Detail	Detail sentences are usually more specific than the topic sentence. In general, detail sentences provide information that is a single or small part of an idea. The words for example, i.e., *that is, first, second, third,* and *finally* often signal a detail sentence.
Support	Most of the detail sentences support, provide examples, prove or document, discuss or elaborate, or point toward the topic sentence in some way.
Answers a Question	To determine if you have identified the topic, switch the sentence around into a question. If the other sentences seem to answer the question you created, then you probably have identified the topic sentence.

Another way that readers determine importance relates to topic sentences. While elementary students mistakenly believe that the main idea is presented in the first sentence of every paragraph, sophisticated readers know that they have to identify the main idea or topic sentence. Collecting several topic sentences and figuring out how they relate to one another helps the reader identify the most salient points of the text. When Ms. Merrill reads a newspaper article with her students, she models determining importance using topic sentences. She uses the newspaper because she knows that the main ideas are unlikely to be presented as the first sentence in each paragraph. Using the tips outlined in Table 4, Ms. Merrill determines the big idea for the text.

Connecting

As we have noted, readers organize information in schemas and hierarchies. This organizational system facilitates connections between and among ideas. As such, readers regularly make connections between texts they are reading and their own life, other things they've read, and the world around them (Keene & Zimmermann, 1997). As Harvey and Goudvis (2000) noted, making connections allows readers to access their prior knowledge and experience. Given that every student has experiences, knowledge, opinions, and emotions that they can draw upon, making connections is often a good starting place for modeling comprehension; however, understand that teacher modeling must ensure that students develop increasingly sophisticated connections and do not repeatedly and continually discuss some personal experience they have had. Table 5 provides a list of questions to facilitate making connections.

Mr. Reese modeled his comprehension strategies with students during a shared reading of *I Am the Mummy Heb-Nefert* (Bunting, 1997). Using a document camera and projector, students followed along as he read. Mr. Reese paused periodically to share his thinking, such as when the author discussed a snake that was tightly coiled and sleeping inside the kitchen basket. He paused and said, "I don't know a lot of people personally who'd want a snake sleeping in their kitchen, but I do know

Table 5 Questions That Facilitate Making Connections	
Type of Connections	**Sample Questions**
Text-to-Self	What does this remind me of in my life? What is this similar to in my life? How is this different from my life? Has something like this ever happened to me? How does this relate to my life? What were my feelings when I read this?
Text-to-Text	What does this remind me of in another book I've read? How is this text similar to other things I've read? How is this different from other books I've read? Have I read about something like this before?
Text-to-World	What does this remind me of in the real world? How is this text similar to things that happen in the real world? How is this different from things that happen in the real world? How did that part relate to the world around me?

Note. From Florida On-Line Reading Professional Development, forpd.ucf.edu/strategies/stratText .html. Reprinted with permission.

from the books we've read so far about ancient Egypt that they had a different relationship with snakes than we do. For example, I remember reading about the snake god Apophis. I also know from the photos and illustrations we've examined that snakes are often thought of as protection. Making these connections helps me put this in context; yes, I guess that people might have had snakes in their houses for protection and to keep the rodents away." This modeling by Mr. Reese allows students to extend the type of connections they make with texts. While most students automatically make connections with their own lives, they need practice with making connections between and among books and the world. Through the modeling their teachers provide, students will begin to see the connections naturally. Over time, they will realize that their understanding of a specific text is really the result of the connections they're making with their background knowledge and experience.

Keep This in Mind

Reading is not simply recognizing meaning that is written *in* a text. Reading requires that meaning be constructed *with* text. In other words, reading is a *transaction* in which the reader brings purposes and life experiences to the text. Comprehension requires attention to what is written, but it also depends upon the reader's background, prior knowledge, purpose, feelings, interests, and needs of the moment. That's why we can read the same text over again and it may have a different meaning. That's also why two people can read the same text, understand the same major points, but get two different ideas from it. Modeling primes the brain for deeper comprehension as students are exposed to, and eventually practice, the behaviors of understanding text.

CHAPTER 4

Word Solving: A Critical Component of Vocabulary Learning

Word knowledge is one of the best predictors of comprehension. It's hard to make meaning of the text when the words are either unknown or not clear. Consider, for example, a sentence used during a presentation on neuroanatomy: "Somites are blocks of dorsal mesodermal cells adjacent to the notochord during vertebrate organogensis." It is clear that the word *somites* is being defined in this sentence, but unless you know a lot about this topic, this sentence is incomprehensible. To understand this sentence, you'd need both background and vocabulary knowledge. Having someone simply define each of the words in this sentence will not result in your developing the ability to understand or to know how to acquire a meaning of these unknown words in the future. We know that simply telling students what words mean does not ensure that they learn them. We'll talk more about depth of word knowledge later in this chapter.

An even worse approach, at least in terms of vocabulary skill development, would be to ask you to look up the words from this sentence on your own. There are simply too many ways that this can go wrong. You might select the wrong definition or use of a word and confuse the meaning. You might skip words you think you already know and miss the point. You might find that some words are defined by words you also don't know. It's just not a sound instructional practice to send students off to look up words on their own. (FYI—Somites are clusters of cells that lie near the back [*dorsal*] side of the developing spinal cord [*notochord*] in an embryo [*vertebrate organogenesis*]. Those cells will eventually become the skin, muscles, and vertebrae of the head and neck.)

Instead, students need to be taught how to solve unknown words. Teachers can do this by modeling word-solving strategies using one of three systems: context clues, word parts, and resources. As we discussed in Chapter 1, modeling is only part of the instructional cycle, and this applies to vocabulary knowledge as well. In this chapter, we focus on where words live in the brain, the importance of words, deep vocabulary instruction, selecting words to teach, and a systematic approach to word learning. We then turn our attention to the modeling strategies used by teachers to ensure that students develop word-solving skills.

Where Words Live in the Brain

The simple answer is that words "live" nearly everywhere in the brain. Reading a single word requires a distributed area of the brain (Fiez & Petersen, 1998). Remember that reading requires the use of structures that have other jobs. Dehaene and Cohen (2007) called this "neuronal recycling" and noted that "cultural inventions" such as reading, writing, and arithmetic "invade evolutionarily older brain circuits and inherit many of their structural constraints" (p. 384). In other words, because we use parts of our brains to read that have evolutionary histories to do other jobs, we have to accept their limitations and the fact that they may go off-task to complete their other responsibilities.

That's not to say that our brains don't have very specific processes for recognizing a word. When we see a word on the printed page, the image transfers from our eyes, through our cranial nerves, through our thalamus, to the occipital lobe. This visual area has highly developed and specialized cells that recognize specific shapes. From the base of the occipital lobe, information transfers to a wider area of the occipital lobe for analysis. Of course, this happens in milliseconds.

There are a number of very important connections between the occipital lobe and the left temporal lobe (for most people), which allows us to recognize the word, both semantically and phonologically. After all, we've all had the experience of being able to recognize a word phonologically without understanding the meaning. That sentence on somites at the beginning of this chapter is a good example. You were able to decode all the words correctly.

But, after reading the words, we had to make some decisions about what we were going to do (or not do) to figure out the meaning of that incomprehensible sentence. That's when our frontal lobes got involved, as this area of the brain controls attention and executive processes. As you toyed with the idea of looking up terms, or rereading for meaning, or taking the word apart, or skipping it all together, that executive portion of your brain was busy at work. Our point is that words live

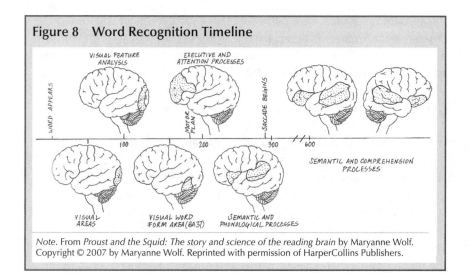

Figure 8 Word Recognition Timeline

Note. From *Proust and the Squid: The story and science of the reading brain* by Maryanne Wolf. Copyright © 2007 by Maryanne Wolf. Reprinted with permission of HarperCollins Publishers.

in quite a few places in the brain but not necessarily simultaneously. There's a whole network that fires up, similar to plugging in a strand of lights on a Christmas tree. A timeline of this word reading process developed by Wolf (2007) can be found in Figure 8.

By now you know that reading requires a well-coordinated chain of events in more than one part of the brain. This certainly parallels the effort we see as our own students read. They marshal lots of resources—background knowledge, prior experience, decoding abilities, word knowledge—to make meaning of what's read. When it is done well, it is akin to watching a master chef at work: Although she may appear to be scrambling about in the kitchen, she is grabbing exactly the right ingredient, precisely the right utensil. In the same regard, we have two specific areas of the brain that are involved in comprehension of words and producing words. Vocabulary, after all, is both understanding words (receptive language) and using them (expressive language). You possess two important areas in your brain that are specifically assigned the duty of processing language.

Wernicke's area, located in the temporal lobe, is responsible for comprehending language. In contrast, **Broca's area** in the frontal lobe is given the job of producing speech (refer again to Figure 1 on page 13). Wernicke's area matures before Broca's, and this should come as no surprise to any parent who has witnessed a toddler's development. Perhaps this is why the "terrible twos" are so difficult: two-year-olds can understand so much but can't express it (Carter, 1998). As the child grows, these two areas establish a connection with one another, a neural pathway called the **arcuate fasciculus**. That pathway plays a critical role in vocabulary development because it allows us to learn new vocabulary when we hear it used by others, and it helps us use it in our own speech. That's why the spoken language element of vocabulary instruction is so important. There seems to be evidence that when this pathway doesn't work well, children experience dyslexia when they learn to read (Silani et al., 2005).

When reading (as opposed to speaking and listening), these two areas work together with a third region called the **angular gyrus**, located in the parietal lobe (refer again to Figure 1 on page 13). The angular gyrus is responsible for recognition of visual symbols critical for reading. We like to think of it as a tollbooth to the visual (occipital) parts of the brain. But it does more than just help the brain recognize a word—there's meaning there, too. As with Wernicke's area (receptive) and Broca's (expressive), this region does something fascinating: It helps the reader see the metaphorical meanings of words and phrases. Ramachandran of the University of California at San Diego (a man some call "the Marco Polo of the brain") demonstrated in 2005 that the angular gyrus is at least partially responsible for understanding metaphors. Without a functioning angular gyrus, you might have known about the 13th century explorer with whom Ramachandran is compared, but you wouldn't have understood the use of *Marco Polo* as a metaphor to describe the work of a 21st century neuroscientist who is mapping heretofore unknown areas of the brain.

What Happens to Words When There Is Damage

We've mentioned what can happen if the connection between Wernicke's and Broca's areas, the arcuate fasciculus, doesn't work well: It can result in dyslexia. As well, damage to either of these areas, such as occurs during stroke or traumatic brain injury, will result in a language-related disability called **aphasia**. The type of language loss depends on the specific location of the damage. For example, people with damage to Broca's area (expressive language) typically speak short, meaningful phrases that are produced with significant effort whereas people with damage to Wernicke's area (receptive language) typically use long sentences that have little or no meaning. They also tend to add unnecessary words and create new nonsense words (neologisms).

Of course, we recognize these are generalizations. Recall from Chapter 1 that Dr. Jill Bolte Taylor recovered all of her language abilities despite significant damage from a stroke and subsequent brain surgery. This is because the human brain has great plasticity, called **neuroplasticity**, that scientists don't fully understand yet. What we do know is that that specific brain functions can relocate as a consequence of normal experience or brain damage and recovery. In some cases, the brain rearranges itself to continue completing tasks. In other cases, it does not.

How the Brain Chooses the "Right" Word Meaning

A surprising finding from neuroscience research concerns multiple word meanings. For example, consider the following newspaper headline: "Kids Make Nutritious Snacks." As the reader, you activated a number of possible word meanings for each of the words and put them together to make sense of the passage. Hopefully you quickly recognized that the author wasn't suggesting that we eat children as a between-meal supplement! However, you *did* consider that meaning before you ruled it out, and of course, that's what makes it funny. If your brain didn't consider all the possible meanings, you would never notice the inadvertent meaning evoked by the lazy headline writer.

Swinney (1979) demonstrated that all known meanings of a word are activated simultaneously when a reader encounters a word. Swinney focused on the word *bug* and demonstrated that readers activated their knowledge of all known meanings of the word (such as insects, spies, Volkswagens, and problems with computer software). His conclusions have a profound impact for vocabulary instruction, namely that we need to understand the varied meanings of words so that we can choose from the range of possible meanings to use the correct one. As he noted, "immediately following occurrence of an ambiguous word all meanings for that word seem to be momentarily accessed during sentence comprehension" (p. 653). This is where vocabulary gets tricky for English-language learners and for anyone who has limited background knowledge. The fewer meanings known, the less likely it is that a student will hit upon the correct and intended usage.

The intricacy of this action was demonstrated by Miller (2001), who assessed the complexity in understanding Robert Frost's poem "Stopping by Woods on a Snowy Evening" using the following excerpt:

> The woods are lovely, dark and deep,
> But I have promises to keep
> And miles to go before I sleep,
> And miles to go before I sleep.

("Stopping by Woods on a Snowy Evening" from *The Poetry of Robert Frost*, edited by Edward Connery Lathem. Copyright © 1923, 1969 by Henry Holt and Company. Copyright © 1951 by Robert Frost. Reprinted with permission of Henry Holt and Company, LLC.)

Simulating what a computer would have to do, Miller determined the range of possible definitions for each word in the 13-word couplet, "But I have promises to keep, and miles to go before I sleep." The word *but* generates 11 meanings and the word *I* generates 3. Based on the assumption that word combinations depend on individual word meanings, the computer would now have 33 (11 × 3) possible compound meanings. Continuing through this process for the entire 13-word couplet, Miller suggests that the computer would discover that there are 3,616,013,016,000 (three trillion six hundred sixteen billion thirteen million sixteen thousand) possible compound meanings or an average of 9.25 meanings per word.

It's easy to see why vocabulary is a critical topic for secondary schools. There simply are thousands of words that students need to know to understand different subject areas. As we saw with the word *bug*, there are multiple meanings for many of these words. We cannot leave vocabulary development to chance if we hope to help students understand what they read. As you will see in the next section, the sheer number of words needed by the time students enter high school is enough to give pause.

The Importance of Words

There is no argument that we are awash in a sea of words at school, both spoken and written. As literacy teachers, we ourselves are consumed with words, and know firsthand of the beauty and power of a well-chosen word. When the noted historian Will Durant said, "Education is a progressive discovery of our own ignorance," he succinctly captured what educators have always known—the more you know, the more you are aware of what you do not yet know. Indeed, it is likely that you selected this book to confirm what you already know, and more important, to discover what you did not yet know. Now let's return to Durant's quote and attend to his word choices. How would this concept suffer without the inclusion of the word *progressive*? How would the power of the quote be diminished if he substituted *continuously moving forward* for *progressive*? Durant crafted a sentence that is pithy and memorable. Further, we would argue that the entire sentence hinges on the word *progressive* because it encapsulates his point—that knowing what you don't know takes time, experience, and learning.

And so it goes with vocabulary itself. Growing a student's vocabulary requires the nurturing of teachers across each grade level, as well as the time and experiences needed to foster vocabulary acquisition that is independent of the teacher. You simply can't be there to teach all 88,500 word families that students will encounter in print by the time they reach high school (Nagy & Anderson, 1984).

Vocabulary acquisition is affected before a child even reaches elementary school. Hart and Risley's (1995) work on language experiences of preschool children illustrated this point in a chilling way. These researches analyzed hour-long in-home recordings gathered from 42 families with infants and toddlers. These recordings were made monthly between the child's 7th and 36th month of life. These families represented a range of socioeconomic backgrounds and were assigned to one of three groups: welfare, working, and professional. They discovered that by age 3, the vocabularies of the children ranged from 500 for the welfare families, to 750 for the working families, to 1100 for the professional families, and that this was in direct correlation to the number of words spoken per hour in the household. Exposure to words is cumulative, of course, and this differential in the volume of words spoken in the household equate to a 30,000,000-word gap by the age of 3. They then followed the progress of these children through third grade, and found that 61% of variance in their verbal ability could be accounted for by the relative exposure to spoken language in the home. Think about what you know about the relationship between Wernicke's area and Broca's area in the brain. All that exposure to spoken language early in life strengthens the neural pathway between these regions.

These two studies (Hart & Risley, 1995; Nagy & Anderson, 1984) are collectively enough to make the fainthearted throw up their hands in despair. After all, the volume of vocabulary students must understand by the time they enter high school is enormous. And what are teachers to do with the children who arrive at our classroom door on the first day of kindergarten with a vocabulary that might be as much as 50% lower than some of their peers? Of course, we wouldn't be writing this book if we didn't think there were ways to help students acquire the vocabulary they need to know. And we know you would find another profession if you didn't think that what you're doing is effective for all your students. Hart and Risley's work, for example, is a strong call for early intervention before the age of 5. Head Start programs, pediatricians, and houses of worship have joined efforts to get books into homes and educate families of the value of talk. And of course, school-aged children benefit from instruction from teachers who understand vocabulary deeply, select it purposefully, and teach it well.

Knowing Different Kinds of Words

The volume of words—88,500—is intimidating but becomes much more manageable when viewed through a categorical system that defines the type of vocabulary. Beck, McKeown, and Kucan (2002) described vocabulary in three categories. Tier 1 words are basic terms that are heard commonly throughout the day, often in spoken language. Look at the previous sentence: *words, are, that, heard, the, day,* and *in* are Tier 1 words. Most students don't need direct instruction in these words, with the exception of those who are new to English. Tier 2 words are those that fill our print world but may be a bit less commonly used orally. These are the "meat and potatoes" of academic language because they offer direction, contrast, and precision to our language. Look again at that sentence that begins with *Tier 1*: the words *basic, terms, commonly, throughout, spoken,* and *language* are examples of Tier 2 words. It is here that Beck and her colleagues advise we expend most of our instructional efforts because these words are pervasive and less likely to be fully understood by our students. The words in the final category, Tier 3, are those that have a very specific, technical meaning. They are comparatively rare and usually tied to a specific content. Returning once more to our same sentence, *Tier 1* is a Tier 3 term because it has a very specific meaning. Admittedly, these categories can break down a bit if overanalyzed. For instance, one could choose to look at *Tier* as a Tier 2 word, and *1* as a Tier 1 word. That's why it is important to remain focused on the purpose of the categories, which is to provide teachers with a tool for making some judgments in selection.

Richard and Jo Anne Vacca have spent their careers looking closely at content area reading, particularly at the secondary level. Their system for describing vocabulary words is particularly useful for middle and high school teachers across subject areas. They categorize words as general, specialized, and technical (Vacca & Vacca, 1999). General vocabulary words are similar to Tier 1 in that they are common to the everyday language and have meanings that are widely held in common. Words such as *book, sunny,* and *write* fall into this category. Specialized vocabulary is trickier for students, especially English-language learners, because the words are used more frequently in print than speech and often possess multiple meanings that are changed by the context. For instance, words such as *filing, focus,* and *secure* are specialized vocabulary. These are vexing because their meaning is bound by syntax and semantics. Consider these six sentences:

1. She was <u>filing</u> her nails in a bored manner while the trial dragged on.
2. The state is <u>filing</u> a writ of habeas corpus.
3. The document camera is out of <u>focus</u>.
4. The <u>focus</u> of this study is on the effects of sunlight on fungus.
5. Monique felt <u>secure</u> in her relationship with D'Vonte.
6. <u>Secure</u> the halyard to the mast cleat on the starboard side.

We will admit that the last sentence is difficult if you don't know anything about sailing. However, our students are often equally puzzled by the context and content of our courses. Your ability to understand *filing* in the second sentence was influenced by your knowledge of law, just as *focus* in the fourth sentence was bound in your understanding of scientific research. Recall what you read about earlier in this chapter regarding the role of the angular gyrus in understanding metaphors. When a reader has only a brief list of possible meanings to run through, it is likely that they will not be able to arrive at the author's intended use of the word.

We have found that the academic word list, developed by Averil Coxhead, is an excellent resource for identifying the specialized vocabulary of secondary schooling. Coxhead analyzed textbooks from all content areas, creating a frequency list. She eliminated the 2,000 most frequently used words in English, then created a list of 570 word families. These lists coincide beautifully with specialized vocabulary and include terms such as *grant, identify, release*, and *major*. Although these words are used profusely throughout textbooks, they don't belong to any one subject and are often overlooked. (A copy of the academic word list is available at http://language.massey.ac.nz/staff/awl/sublist2.shtml.)

Vacca and Vacca (1999) described a third category of vocabulary they call technical. Similar to Tier 3 words, they are words and terms that are closely associated with a particular content and have a precise meaning. *Sine* and *cosine* in calculus, *Sylvian fissure* in biology, *Glorious Revolution* in world history, even *halyard* in sailing all are examples of technical vocabulary. As secondary teachers, we tend to focus quite a bit of instruction on these terms, perhaps because they are near and dear to our content. By all means, these need to be taught. However, general, specialized, and technical vocabulary should not bear an equal weight in your instructional day. It is the specialized vocabulary that poses the most difficulty for students and should therefore have a bit more of your attention. Which brings us to our next point: teaching vocabulary deeply.

Deep Vocabulary Instruction

Thus far, we have spent quite a bit of time discussing vocabulary as words when in truth it is far more that that—it is concepts. Therefore, modeling understanding and use of vocabulary must ultimately be bound in concept development, not just mastery of isolated words. We use the research on the teaching of concepts to inform our instruction of vocabulary. Tennyson and Cocchiarella (1986) examined the research base on concept development to recommend a five-part process for instructional design: (1) label and define, (2) contextualize, (3) give a best example, (4) elaborate on attributes, and (5) provide strategy information. These components translate well to the realm of vocabulary development. Let's explore each of these steps using a Tier 2, specialized word: *simulate.*

1. *Label and define.* Students first need to be able to accurately assign a label and a short meaning to an unfamiliar term. When encountering the word *simulate*, the teacher can pause to say, "That means imitate, to make something like another thing."

2. *Contextualize.* Once it's defined, students benefit from grounding the term within the intended usage by the author: "Let me reread that sentence. 'The state Disaster Preparedness team simulated an oil spill to test emergency preparedness.' Since *simulate* means to imitate, I know that the oil spill was not real."

3. *Give a best example.* This is a time to provide solid examples of the way in which the word is used. The best examples are often connections to something with which the students are already familiar: "I've heard of simulations before, like in video games that recreate an environment. I know that's where the Sim City program got its name."

4. *Elaborate on attributes.* Contrastive examples help learners to understand what something is and is not. Therefore, more examples as well as non-examples will round out their understanding: "*Simulate* means to imitate, but usually in a fake kind of way. It is not recreating something so that it is exactly the same. It wouldn't make sense for them to really spill huge amounts of oil just to test their ability."

5. *Provide strategy information.* Now point out to students the strategies you used to get to the meaning of the word: "When I looked at *simulate*, I noticed how much it reminded me of the word *similar*, which means almost, but not quite, the same. I also made the connection to something I was familiar with—the Sim City software program. When I run across an unfamiliar word, I think about words I am reminded of."

Of course, you can't (and shouldn't) do this with every word. Selecting the right words on which to spend direct instructional time is another facet of the complexities of vocabulary instruction. In the next section, we describe a decision-making model for choosing vocabulary words for special attention.

Selecting Words to Teach

This is perhaps the greatest conundrum that plagues teachers of vocabulary: How do you know which is the *right* word to select for your students' attention? Given the wide range of words present in any text, how can you be sure you've chosen well? We'd like to take a slightly different approach to this debate. As we described in the previous section, people learn by example and non-example, and this is borne out in the research on concept development and instruction on critical attributes (Tennyson & Cocchiarella, 1986). Let's first examine the most common mistakes made when choosing words to teach, then discuss a decision-making model for selecting vocabulary wisely for attention during modeling.

Common Mistakes When Choosing Instructional Words

Choosing words is a difficult task, and we've made our share of mistakes over the years. Let's look closer at three common mistakes that are made when selecting words.

Mistake #1: Choosing the "big" words. It seems as though our eyes are drawn toward the unusual. This can be useful when shopping for a new outfit to wear to a fancy event, but it can be problematic when selecting a word for instruction. Rare words are rare for a reason—they occur relatively infrequently in spoken and written language. For example, the word *wallowed* only appears once in the book *Owen and Mzee* (Hatkoff, Hatkoff, & Kahumbu, 2006). It can be tempting to spend time on this word because it is unusual, but in truth it is enough to allow the context of the story and the description of the hippopotamus enjoying standing in the water to define the word for readers.

Mistake #2: Choosing too many words. As teachers, we love the ideas that come spilling off the printed page and are eager to share them with our students. This is especially true when it comes to informational text with its dense lexical units. A reading about trees, for example, might contain eight or ten big, glamorous terms per page. But this can be far too many to model during a reading. Instead, focus your choices on just a few powerful words that allow you to build word knowledge that can be transferred to other words and texts.

Mistake #3: Overlooking the "little" words. As we noted earlier, words fall into categories depending on their function within the curriculum. Those Tier 3, or technical vocabulary, words may capture our attention, but they can't be focused on at the expense of Tier 2, specialized vocabulary. Imagine the student who learns about *photosynthesis* but doesn't understand that it is a *process*.

Decision-Making Model for Selecting Words

How then should one make decisions about selecting words for instructional consideration? We have long used a series of reflective questions inspired by Graves and Slater (1996) to make determinations about vocabulary. Naturally, two teachers teaching the same content will arrive at slightly different lists; however, our experience in working with departments and grade-level teams shows that the overlap is far greater than the differences.

Representative: Is it essential to understand the text? It's hard to imagine understanding Edgar Allan Poe's short story "The Purloined Letter" without knowing what purloined means. In this case, it is well worth the time to provide instruction about this term upfront.

Repeatability: Will the word be used again in this text or in this course? If yes, the word may well be worth teaching. If no, you may want to just explain it and move on. As mentioned, *wallowed* in *Owen and Mzee* (Hatkoff, Hatkoff, & Kahumbu, 2006) is one such non-example and is not worthy of significant instructional focus.

Transportable: Can it be used in other content areas? Here's where that specialized vocabulary returns. As we have described, these words are often orphaned because they are not claimed by any one content area. We recommend that grade levels select a bank of specialized vocabulary, especially those that frequently appear on tests (*identify, describe, analyze, simplify,* and the like) for attention during modeling. This draws the students' attention to the versatility of these terms across the curriculum.

Contextual analysis: Can students arrive at the meaning through context? If yes, then the word may not need direct instruction; although, it could be a good candidate for modeling how you use contextual analysis to understand the word.

Structural analysis: Can students arrive at the meaning through structure? Many words are members of a word family, and word meaning is altered through prefixes and suffixes. If the meaning of the word in question is easily determined through structural analysis, it may not warrant lots of instructional attention. However, if students need to understand how structure informs a host of words, then it can be useful during modeling.

Cognitive load: How many words are reasonable to teach? By any measure, this is a judgment call. There are several factors at play, including the needs of the students and the overall length of the piece. During read-alouds and shared readings, we rarely venture beyond five words to highlight and typically we only focus on two or three words. More than that interrupts the flow too much, and students reach cognitive overload. In addition, a draft list is a good way to keep oneself in check. If the list is too long, then reexamine whether the text is too difficult.

A Systematic Approach to Word Learning

As we have noted, students need to be taught to solve unknown words. In keeping with the information we presented in Chapter 1, teachers can help students create neural networks by exposing thinking and facilitating students' use of the approaches that are modeled. Over time, and with practice, these networks of word knowledge, word retrieval, and word use are strengthened. Of course we can't see these networks, but we do see students who use their knowledge of vocabulary during reading and writing activities.

We, as teachers, can't leave vocabulary development to chance. There are simply too many words with too many definitions to take a "wait and see" approach. We also can't teach every word or word meaning that students will need. There isn't time to directly teach all of these words. And, as we'll see, it isn't necessary as students need to be taught how to solve words and not just the definitions of lots of words.

Modeling Word Solving

The first component of a systematic approach to vocabulary skill development is modeling word solving. Students need multiple examples across content areas of how to figure out words from context or by using morphology. As we show in the section that follows, students need concrete examples of the thinking required to process word meanings, the use of background knowledge, and the range of possibilities presented by the context.

For example, Ms. Lockwood modeled her thinking of vocabulary while reading a *New York Times* article (Nagourney, 2007). The opening sentence of the article used the term *dementia* but did not provide context clues. She read aloud the first sentence: "People with more years of schooling appear to suffer the symptoms of dementia later than others who have it—but once it does come, it proceeds more quickly, researchers say." She then said, "One of the things I understand is that people who go to school longer, like into college, seem to have less of something called *dementia*. *Dementia* doesn't sound positive, but it's not defined here. I remember the Dementors in the Harry Potter books, and they were no good. I also have heard people say *demented* meaning confused or strange. But look, I can click right here [on the word *dementia*] and find out more. I'll use this resource. Oh, wow, there's a ton of information about this."

In this case, Ms. Lockwood modeled the connections she made between an unknown word and her background knowledge. She also modeled using resources to figure out word meanings. Again, the key to modeling is not to focus only on the meaning of a specific word in the reading, but rather how to find word meanings while reading. In other words, it's about teaching students procedures for word solving that they can use in their own reading.

Wide Reading

One of the ways that students extend their vocabulary knowledge is through reading. While reading, students apply their developing word-solving skills. In addition to reading lots of words they know and use regularly, readers encounter a number of words that they know, but that are used in new contexts or with slightly different meanings. Reading introduces readers to people they've never met and an opportunity to visit places they've never been. Along the way, they encounter words for these places, people, and experiences. As Cunningham and Stanovich (1998) noted, "reading has cognitive consequences that extend beyond its immediate task of lifting meaning from a particular passage" (p. 1). These experiences build and reinforce understanding of words in the brain. In other words, reading widely builds background knowledge, and students who read more have larger vocabularies and tend to score higher on assessments.

Of course, students have to read things they *can* read for this to be effective. As Allington (2002) noted, "you can't learn much from books you can't read" (p. 16). As we saw in the sentence that opened this chapter, reading things that are too hard doesn't facilitate learning. Students, like scientists or historians, need to read a lot from a lot of different sources to understand the content. You can't imagine that a scientist would read from one source, right? Similarly, historians would be laughed out of their meetings if they reported only reading one perspective. It stands to reason then that our students need to read widely *and* read things that they can read.

Consider the study of ancient Roman times, common in sixth-grade classrooms in the United States. Textbooks provide an overview of the content, complete with visuals and other text supports. As such, they are a critical resource for the young historian trying to understand these people, far away and long ago. The teacher can use the textbook for modeling thinking or for groups to read during productive group work (see Chapter 1). To develop a sophisticated understanding of ancient Roman civilization, students need to read widely (and from books they can read).

Mr. Blythe is a teacher who provides his students with exactly this opportunity by making available a number of books on ancient Rome during this unit. Students select books to read and read daily during class. Mr. Blythe knows that this builds students' background knowledge and facilitates word learning. He also knows that repeated exposure to targeted words in different contexts increases the likelihood that students will learn them. It's a simple matter of understanding the brain: Novel stimuli are more interesting. Thus, reading widely maintains interest. Along the way, students are exposed to words that they connect with concepts. Because they're reading books they can read, the words students encounter build and reinforce the neural networks we've talked about. When they do encounter an unfamiliar word or a word used in an unfamiliar way, students deploy the strategies that have been modeled for them. The only thing that is left to do is consolidate word knowledge, which simply means that word meanings are transferred to long-term memory. To do this, students have to work with words.

Working With Words

Given the effort expended to model the use of a vocabulary word, it would make little sense if students didn't have an opportunity to then apply the word in engaging ways. We know that a necessary factor in word learning is multiple exposures (Blachowicz & Fisher, 2000), and that meaningful vocabulary activities that require students to use targeted words in oral and written language can consolidate their understanding.

Concept sorts. Vocabulary sorting activities have long held a strong reputation among elementary educators, and with some adjustments for developmental appropriateness, can be equally viable at the secondary level. Traditionally students sort words written on cards or small slips of paper according to attributes or characteristics. These can be defined in advance by the teacher (a closed sort) or determined by the student (an open sort). In the example shown in Figure 9, a student in an English class

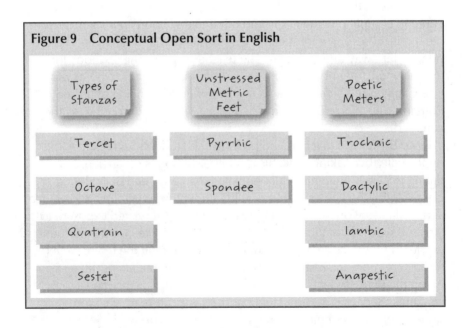

Figure 9   Conceptual Open Sort in English

Types of Stanzas	Unstressed Metric Feet	Poetic Meters
Tercet	Pyrrhic	Trochaic
Octave	Spondee	Dactylic
Quatrain		Iambic
Sestet		Anapestic

Figure 10   Semantic Feature Analysis in World History

	Leader Killed	Supported by Military	Supported by the People	Resulted in More Freedoms
American Revolution	−	+	+	+
French Revolution	+	−	+	+
Haitian Revolution	−	−	+	+
Russian Revolution	+	−	+	−

sorted terms according to patterns she identified for herself. Sorts are useful because they give students opportunities to construct schemas.

Semantic feature analysis. This instructional routine invites students to consider the attributes of a set of related terms and to determine how they are similar and different from one another. We like to think of this as a two-way sort, going both down the columns and across the rows. Semantic feature analysis encourages students to think about the relationships between concepts and to determine whether particular attributes are a feature of the term (Anders & Bos, 1986). Figure 10 presents a semantic feature analysis used in a world history class.

Text impressions. Traditionally this is done in advance of a reading to activate background knowledge and foster predictions. A list is developed consisting of a mixture of vocabulary from the reading (primarily specialized and technical vocabulary). Students then use the list of words to write a paragraph that links all of the words together. We also like to use them after a reading in order for students to develop summaries. As with those done before a reading, we instruct students to use the terms in the order they appear on the list. Therefore, careful consideration must be given to the way the list is composed.

Analogies. Analogous thinking raises the intellectual stakes considerably, as these are considered to be among the most complex word relationships. However, they can be powerful exercises for students to stretch their ability to manipulate words. Analogies are usually taught in the form of *A* is to *B* as *C* is to *D*. For example, *man* is to *woman* as *boy* is to *girl*. Note that the emphasis is not only on the relationship between *A* and *B*, but also on the commonality of the relationships between *A* and *B* and between *C* and *D*. Many teachers use these to stress grammatical relationships, such as the following: *Who* is to *whom* as *they* is to *them*.

Words can also be conceptually analogous, as biology teacher Mr. Bonine taught his students in a unit about the immune system. He used the analogy of a police force to describe the work of various cells in fighting a virus. He compared natural killer cells to police officers, who are the first responders to a crime scene. He also described the work of dendritic cells as analogous to a police detective—they arrive later and collect virus fragments (evidence) to carry to the T cells and B cells. Later, when asked to write an analogy to describe this function, students correctly wrote, "Natural killer cells are to police officers as dendritic cells are to detectives."

Modeling Word Solving

As we have noted, modeling of vocabulary at the secondary level should focus on word-solving strategies and not just word meanings. We have to teach students what to do when they come to unknown words. In general, word solving can be categorized in two ways: (1) outside-the-word strategies that require the use of context clues and (2) inside-the-word strategies that require using parts of words, such as affixes, roots, and cognates. When these two systems don't help, students need to know how to use resources that can help them figure out word meanings.

Context Clues: Outside-the-Word Strategies

Readers use a number of clues provided by the author to understand unknown words. Of course, most readers use context clues, or their outside-the-word strategies, automatically as they read (Nagy, Anderson, & Herman, 1985). Teachers can model the use of context clues to figure out unknown or confusing words by focusing embedded definitions, synonyms, antonyms, comparisons, contracts, descriptions, and examples.

During her shared reading of *Coming on Home Soon* (Woodson, 2004), Ms. Donaldson read the line "When she put her dress into the satchel, I held my breath" (p. 1) then said, "I'm not sure what a satchel is. I'll read this page and check out the picture. If I can't figure it out from this information, I'll ask someone for some help." A few sentences later, she read the line "Mama folded another dress and put it in the bag" (p. 1) and said, "Another dress in the bag? She already put a dress in the satchel. I bet that a satchel is a special kind of bag, but it looks like a suitcase in the picture. I'm going to reread this page with the word suitcase in place of both *bag* and *satchel* to see if this makes sense. . . . [Rereads sentences.] Yes, it does. So there's another word for a suitcase, a special kind of bag for traveling."

Mr. Patterson, a seventh-grade teacher, while reading from the history textbook, noted that the author had provided a "right there" meaning for the word. He said, "Let me read that again. 'Romans also learned from Greek science. A Greek doctor named Galen brought many medical ideas to Rome. For example, he emphasized the importance of anatomy, the study of body structure.' I know that anatomy is the study of the structure of the body because the definition was embedded right there in the text. I'm always on the lookout for help the author provides. I'm also thinking about the connections between the Greeks and the Romans. To summarize what I've read so far in the chapter, the Romans benefited significantly from the learnings of the Greeks. On your interactive note pages, list a few things that the Romans learned from the Greeks and then talk with your group about these things."

Both of these teachers demonstrate the ways in which readers use context clues to determine word meaning. Context clues come in several types, including

- *Antonym or contrast clue.* A word or phrase is clarified using an alternative or opposite meaning.
- *Restatement or synonym clue.* A word or phrase is restated in more common terms or a synonym is provided.
- *Definition or example clue.* A word or phrase is defined shortly after its use or an example is provided.
- *Inference or general knowledge clue.* A word or phrase is explained in previous or subsequent sentences or the author relies on the reader's common knowledge.

Table 6 lists four common types of context clues with example sentences and common signal words that help the reader know that context clues are present.

In addition to the four types of context clues presented in Table 6, sometimes punctuation or print style serves as a context clue. Readers

Table 6   Types of Context Clues

Type of Context Clue	Definition	Signals	Examples
Antonym or Contrast Clue	Phrases or words that indicate opposite	But, in contrast, however, instead of, unlike, yet	Unlike his *quiet and low key* family, Brad is *garrulous*.
Definition or Example Clue	Phrases or words that define or explain	Is defined as, means, the term, [a term in boldface or italics] set off with commas	*Sedentary* individuals, people who are not very active, often have diminished health.
General Knowledge	The meaning is derived from the experience and background knowledge of the reader; "common sense" and logic.	The information may be something basically familiar to you	Lourdes is always sucking up to the boss, even in front of others. That *sycophant* just doesn't care what others think of her behavior.
Restatement or Synonym Clue	Another word or phrase with the same or a similar meaning is used.	In other word, that is, also known as, sometimes called, or	The *dromedary*, commonly called a camel, stores fat in its hump.

Note. Developed by Sharon Teuben-Rowe, Montgomery College, Tacoma Park, Maryland, USA. Used with permission.

can be taught that to infer meaning from quotation marks (showing the word has a special meaning), dashes (added information about the topic), parentheses or brackets (enclosing a definition or example), and italics or boldface (showing the word will be defined in the glossary). Consider the following examples of punctuation use in describing a specific neural structure, the **amygdala**:

- The amygdala, an almond-shaped groups of neurons located in the temporal lobes of the brain, has a primary role in the processing and memory of emotional reactions.

- The amygdala is also involved in the slow formation of long-term information storage (the duration of long-term memory storage can be infinite) called *memory consolidation*.

- The amygdala is considered part of the limbic system—the part of the brain that regulates human moods and emotions—and is one of the sites where the parasite that causes toxoplasmosis takes residence.

Even if you have little background knowledge about the amygdala, you could use those punctuation and print styles to figure out that it (1) is located in the temporal lobes, (2) consolidates memory, and (3) has a role in regulating mood and emotion. Your knowledge of those text devices allowed you to efficiently locate context clues that provided you with vocabulary knowledge. When these opportunities present themselves in a reading, model how you use them to determine meaning of unfamiliar words.

Word Parts: Inside-the-Word Strategies

In addition to context clues, there are a number of inside-the-word strategies students can use to figure out word meanings. These include prefixes, suffixes, roots, bases, word families, and cognates. Word part lessons are often quick and somewhat explanatory. For example, Ms. Thibodeaux, while reading from a textbook noted, "Carnivore reminds me of *carne* in Spanish meaning 'meat.' It also reminds me of *carne asada*, a kind of meat, but that just makes me hungry. So, I use carne to remind me that carnivores eat meat."

Mr. Drexel, a science teacher, paused on the word *evaporation* while reading about the water cycle and said, "I know how to remember this word. It has vapor in it and that means steam, like to vaporize. I also know that -*tion* is a process. So, evaporation is a process that allows the water to disappear into the steam or air."

While reading from a magazine article about war wounds, Mr. Muller came across the word malodorous and said, "Now here's a great word: *malodorous*. Say this wonderful word with me: *malodorous*. I know that the prefix *mal-* is bad and that *odor* has to do with smell and the suffix -*ous* means full of or having the characteristic of. So putting it together *malodorous* is being full of bad smells. Isn't that a delicious word? Now, instead of saying it's *stinky* or *foul*, you can say *malodorous*. The malodorous locker room, the malodorous streets filled with refuse, plants with malodorous bouquets. You try it, you use the word [pauses while students talk together]. Just beautiful!"

Table 7 provides a list of the most common prefixes and suffixes. These should certainly be modeled until they are familiar to students. Of

Table 7   The 20 Most Frequent Affixes in Printed School English

Rank	Prefix	% of All Prefixed Words	Suffix	% of All Suffixed Words
1	un-	26	-s, -es	31
2	re-	14	-ed	20
3	in-, im-, il-, ir- (not)	11	-ing	14
4	dis-	7	-ly	7
5	en-, em-	4	-er, -or (agent)	4
6	non-	4	-ion, -tion, -ation, -ition	4
7	in-, im- (in)	3	-able, -ible	2
8	over-	3	-al, -ial	1
9	mis-	3	-y	1
10	sub-	3	-ness	1
11	pre-	3	-ity, -ty	1
12	inter-	3	-ment	1
13	fore-	3	-ic	1
14	de-	2	-ous, -eous, -ious	1
15	trans-	2	-en	1
16	super-	1	-er (comparative)	1
17	semi-	1	-ive, -ative, -tive	1
18	anti-	1	-ful	1
19	mid-	1	-less	1
20	under- (too little)	1	-est	1
	All others	3	All others	1

Note. From White, T. G., Sowell, J., & Yanagihara, A. (1989). Teaching elementary students to use word-part clues. *The Reading Teacher, 42,* 302–309. Reprinted with permission.

course, these aren't the only affixes that deserve attention. As students get older, they come in contact with words with affixes that are much rarer as is the case with the word *malodorous* above. Based on the explanation they received about *mal-*, students might be able to make an educated guess about *malcontent*, *malevolent*, *malnutrition*, and *malicious*.

Breaking a word apart to analyze its structure is easy when the affix or the root is obvious, but many words don't wear their derivations so boldly. Wolf (2007) explained,

> Words like "muscle" teach the way our words carry an entire history within them.... For example, the silent "c" in "muscle" may seem unnecessary, but in fact it visibly connects the word to its origin, the Latin root *musculus*, from which we have kindred words as "muscular" and "musculature".... The silent "c" of "muscle" therefore, visually conveys the morphemic aspect of English. (p. 42)

We know that it's not always possible to be an expert in breaking words apart, so we rely on a bit of help to supply the information we need. We especially like *The Dictionary of Word Roots and Combining Forms* (Borror, 1988), a small and handy dictionary of alphabetically arranged roots. This book has long been considered a must on the shelves of medical students, teachers, and writers, and we find it easier to use than many of the Internet-based dictionaries. This is useful when trying to figure out why certain words are constructed in such seemingly baffling ways. This brings us to our last aspect of modeling vocabulary— using resources to determine meaning.

Resources

When outside-the-word and inside-the-word strategies fail, teachers can model the use of resources. Most commonly, this involves asking another person. For example, when she came across the word *atmosphere* on a page with no context clues, Ms. Green said, "I'm not sure about this word. I can't really get it from context. I'll try some resources. Well, there's no glossary to help me out. I guess I'll call Ms. Johnson next door and ask her if she knows what this word really means." After finishing her call, she told the class what Mrs. Johnson told her about the vocabulary word. Using the analogy of the television show *Who Wants to Be a Millionaire,* Ms. Green went on to say, "I know it's not always practical to 'phone a friend' in school, but you've got lots of ways to check with others right here in class. Sometimes solving a word can be as simple as asking someone sitting near you."

Help from resources can also arrive in the form of dictionaries, glossaries, and Web-based references. While reading *Patrol: An American Soldier in Vietnam* (Myers, 2002), seventh-grade teacher Ms. Francis stopped on the page that read, "Two clicks away, there are flashes of gunfire. Two clicks is the distance of my enemy" (p. 15). She then paused and said, "I've heard of clicks before but mostly about the Internet. You know, click on this page and stuff. I think I want to know what this is, and I don't have any context clues to use to figure it out. I'm going to look it up really quick." Turning to the computer, Ms. Francis typed *measurement click* into the search engine while she said, "I know that it's a measurement because the author says distance, so I guess I did have a little bit of context help." Ms. Francis selected a couple of websites that define click, including *The History Channel*, which notes that click has two common definitions: (1) 1 click = 1 kilometer and (2) the adjustments on the sight of a weapon for elevation and wind. She then says, "So the enemy is about two kilometers away. That's not too far, but far enough to feel a bit safer. I'll reread this page with my new understanding."

Keep This in Mind

Modeling word solving is an important component of vocabulary learning. Without examples of word solving across disciplines, students are not likely to develop their independent word leaning skills. We know that students tend to overgeneralize, at least at first, things that their teachers model. This can be good in the development of habits such as making predictions. It's not such a good thing when the overgeneralization reduces the use of a habit or results in less reading.

For example, a popular approach for dealing with an unknown word, which has been printed on several commercially available classroom posters, is to skip it. If skipping words was overgeneralized, students would not develop the other habits required of word solving. As such, we don't think that the skip it strategy should be modeled for the whole class. Instead teachers may talk about skipping words, rereading, and finding meaning other ways with small groups of students so that they understand the strategic use of this approach.

The point of modeling is to develop students' habits by providing them with an example that they can use on their own. As such, we should model effective approaches for solving unknown words and not simply skipping words that are difficult. This modeling allows our students to see for themselves what is happening in our own brains. The very fact that word knowledge comes together from several regions of the brain should be further support for modeling as a tool for teaching vocabulary. To "know" a word, we must recognize it phonologically, process its syntactic qualities, and rapidly rifle through every possible meaning of the word, comparing it to the context. By modeling how we make these decisions, we let students in on the secret—that words don't live in isolation, but rather exist as players in a dance of ideas choreographed by the writer. The ultimate goal is not to memorize a list of words, but rather to have word-solving skills ready to deploy with automaticity so that when students read independently, they can deploy these word-solving skills with automaticity.

CHAPTER 5

Text Structures:
Guidance for Readers
That Facilitates Memory

M any of us have had the experience at one time or another when we bought a book that was too difficult. What made it so hard? Chances are we were motivated to learn about the topic, and presumably that factored into our choice in the first place. It's doubtful that we failed to preview the text—most of us wouldn't dream of purchasing a book without looking at the back cover, the inside flap, and maybe a few online reviews in advance of the purchase. Yet when we got home and began reading, we figured out pretty quickly that this was not a good fit. As we have discussed in previous chapters, vocabulary and background knowledge undoubtedly played a big role in comprehension. But there were other subtleties at work: The text itself may not have been very friendly (we teachers usually refer to it as inconsiderate text). And as we read, the paragraphs became more impenetrable; there were so many concepts packed into each sentence that the words began to swim on the page. Defeated, we trudged back to the bookstore to find an easier one—preferably one with the phrase "for Dummies" in the title.

Nancy had this experience a few years ago when she wanted to learn more about Buddhism. She had a few friends who were Buddhists, and she had picked up a fair amount of extraneous information and vocabulary over the years. So one day she headed off to the world religions section of the bookstore and found a likely candidate. But when she began to read, the text quickly went right over her head. All that business about the Four Noble Truths—was that different from the Eightfold Path?—and what exactly is an "ornament of the mind"? Fortunately, on her next trip to the bookstore, she found *Buddhism for Dummies* (Landlaw & Bodian, 2003), setting her rightly on her own Eightfold Path.

While we think it's ironic to suggest that anything about Buddhism is less than considerate, in this case Nancy noted that the first text she chose didn't have many of the elements she needed as a novice to the content. It didn't use a lot of signal words to cue her about the text structure; for example, she would have understood more if there were a sentence that said, "In *contrast* to the Four Noble Truths, which describe the accepted truths of this life, the Eightfold Path is the way in which a Buddhist chooses to live a noble life." These explicit signals of the structures would give the text a sense of coherence as concepts are built one upon the other. The second book she chose did a better job of offering explicit text structures and coherence.

There's a very good reason why a more coherent text, with lots of signal words to make relationships between concepts clear, results in higher levels of comprehension. When the reader doesn't have to expend so much attention on surface-level meaning, her working memory is freed to do more of the deep comprehension the text demands. In this chapter, we discuss four elements of reading as they relate to the text and memory: (1) What makes a text "considerate"? (2) What is working memory, and how can we reduce demand on it when reading? (3) What is the relationship between working memory and text structure? and (4) How do we facilitate long-term memory? We then give some examples of modeling the use of text structure in various classroom settings.

Considerate Text: Selecting Texts With the Reader in Mind

Armbruster (1996) coined the term *considerate texts* to describe texts that facilitate comprehension and learning from reading. Her research and the research of others (e.g., Boscolo & Mason, 2003; Chambliss, 1994; Kobayashi, 2002; Meyer, 2003; Mosenthal & Kirsch, 1992; Tyree, Fiore, & Cook, 1994) suggests that there are three overlapping features of text that contribute to comprehension and learning: structure, coherence, and audience appropriateness. Let's examine each of these in greater detail and review current research on each of these factors.

Structure

There is significant evidence that the ways in which the ideas or topics are arranged and related has a great impact on students' comprehension

(Bakken & Whedon, 2002; Ciardiello, 2002; Parsons, 2000). The most common informational text structures include

- *Description.* A list of information
- *Compare and contrast.* Noted similarities and differences between two concepts
- *Temporal sequence.* How events change or remain the same over time
- *Cause and effect.* Causal relationships
- *Problem and solution.* A situation or issue and how it is resolved

There are a number of ways that authors can use text structure to help readers make meaning. Selecting texts that include these characteristics helps students read for information. First, texts can provide headings and subheadings that guide readers through information (see Chapter 6 for a more detailed discussion of text features). Second, text can use signals or hints about how a text is structured such as introductions, specific words that convey the structure (such as *first, second,* and *third* for description and *because, since,* or *as a result* for cause and effect), learning objectives that indicate the structure, and margin information to aid the reader. And third, text can be supplemented with graphic support such as the use of Venn diagrams, structured overviews, semantic feature analyses, maps, and the like. Taken together, these key elements ensure that students learn the content being presented in the text as well as how to read informational texts in the future.

Coherence

The second factor that ensures that texts are considerate of their readers relates to the idea that concepts, phenomenon, and events must be explained. We call this coherence because readers need the text to provide connections internally, in a systematic or logical way. Again, there is significant evidence that coherence is an important consideration and one that influences understanding (McNamara & Kintsch, 1996; Meyer, 2003; Sanders, 1997).

Like structure, there are a number of features that can be included in a text to specifically address the issue of text coherence. Again, these features can be assessed before texts are selected. First, the main ideas can be explicitly stated in the chapter openings and in an obvious place as each section begins. Second, the information found within a paragraph or section can be clearly connected back to the main idea. Third, the events should have a logical order, and events and topics should have an obvious relationship between them. Fourth, the text should provide readers with clear references and referents and not use ambiguous pronouns. And finally, topics should transition smoothly to facilitate remembering.

Audience Appropriateness

The final factor that makes a text considerate concerns the extent to which the material corresponds with the knowledge of the intended audience. In other words, audience appropriateness is a measure of how well the text matches the students' probable background and prior knowledge, which we know are two important considerations when considering text difficulty. Textbook writers must consider how much information students already know and should "elaborate new concepts sufficiently to be meaningful to readers and to facilitate learning" (Armbruster, 1996, p. 54). The research on audience appropriateness is particularly strong (Alexander, Schallert, & Hare, 1991; Heffernan, 2003).

As with structure and coherence, there are a number of elements that can be included in a text to address the issue of audience appropriateness. First, the authors or editors (as well as the person selecting the text to teach) can evaluate the conceptual density (the number of new concepts per unit of text) to ensure that there is a balance between addressing the core content standards while keeping it from becoming too dense. Second, the text can include more information about fewer topics thus allowing a precise focus on the content to be covered. In doing so, the texts can use, validate, and extend the information students already have about a topic. Third, the text can specifically address common misconceptions readers have. These misconceptions are often the source of audience mismatch as students may not be able to integrate new information unless their misunderstandings are specifically addressed.

In sum, the accessibility of a text, or whether or not it is considerate of readers, has a profound impact on cognitive demand, memory, and thus comprehension. Texts selected for instruction should include specific structural features to guide readers. Texts must be coherent and allow readers to follow the logical flow of the book and the text must be written in such a way that the audience is considered and addressed. Combined with high quality teaching (Simpson & Nist, 2000), these three text factors are important considerations worthy of attention and discussion.

As we stated earlier in this chapter, the use of the principles of considerate text, especially signal words to support structure, has a larger purpose. These elements free up working memory in the brain so that the reader can focus attention on the more interesting aspects of the content, rather than on slogging through the bog of dense text.

Reducing the Demand on Working Memory

Memory has served as a source of fascination for thousands of years. In the oral tradition, the ability to memorize and accurately repeat historical accounting and family genealogy was highly prized. Indeed, Socrates protested the use of a writing system, fearing that the change from an oral to a written society would negatively affect the intellectual life of the Greeks (Wolf, 2007). During the 20th century, scientific attention on the source and function of memory gradually revealed more understanding of this aspect of thought and cognition. Studies in the 1950s on digit span (the ability to recall a string of unrelated numbers) yielded results that suggested that most adults could recall an average of seven to nine digits (Miller, 1956). This period also marked the emergence of short-term memory as a way to distinguish information that could be retained for a short period of time (such as remembering a phone number) and more permanent memory.

The term working memory was coined in the 1970s by Baddeley and Hitch to describe the function of a portion of memory that retains information for more than a few seconds. They described three components—a **phonological loop** (such as when you mutter the phone number to yourself until you dial the phone), a **visual-spatial sketchpad** that holds nonlinguistic information in storage (such as knowing what it looks like behind you after you have looked over your shoulder), and a **central executive function** that oversees the other two systems (Baddeley & Hitch, 1974). The purpose of working memory, Baddeley and Hitch proposed, was to store information for long enough that it could be manipulated. It appears that working memory is the key difference between the word-by-word reading of beginners and true fluency, the point at which decoding, vocabulary, and comprehension work together in concert. Novice readers must dedicate precious working memory to the tasks of decoding and surface reading. As automaticity increases and working memory is no longer needed to perform these tasks, the reader is able to devote attention to concepts and ideas across a longer chunk of text. Read the first sentence of the short story "Salvador Late or Early" by Sandra Cisneros (1991) to see how your working memory functions:

> Salvador with eyes the color of caterpillar, Salvador of the crooked hair and crooked teeth, Salvador whose name the teacher cannot remember, is a boy who is no one's friend, runs along somewhere in that vague direction where homes are the color of bad weather, lives behind a raw wood doorway, shakes the sleepy brothers awake, ties their shoes, combs their hair with water, feeds them milk and cornflakes from a tin cup in the dim dark of the morning. (p. 10)

This sentence is 80 words long and contains a long string of descriptors about Salvador. But because you are a fluent reader, you are able to hold all these ideas in your head as you read: Salvador is a boy, his teacher can't remember his name, he lives in a rundown house, and he helps to care for his younger brothers. Perhaps you thought of a child you know who reminds you of Salvador. In addition, you may have analyzed those 80 words for stylistic choices, noting that perhaps Cisneros chose to write this way to convey the many responsibilities and many facets of Salvador. If you are a fan of the author, you may have even compared this excerpt to other writings by her. Because your working memory was freed from the task of having to decode, make choices about how to deal with punctuation, and think about the vocabulary, you were able to engage in more sophisticated tasks. This is precisely what Afflerbach et al. (2008) meant when they suggested that, over time, strategies can become skills as they move to the level of automatic action. We are able to manipulate the information across the sentence using the visual-spatial sketchpad because we can hold onto the visual information as we read, and the central executive function directs what happens in this temporary storage system—our working memory.

The Relationship Between Working Memory and Text Structure

As you can imagine, working memory performs a critical function in the brain's ability to read and to manipulate information, especially as the learner gains automaticity, thereby improving the efficiency of working memory. It is a factor in understanding text structure (which is not something to which young readers can really attend) because the brain is able to notice the signal words and complex idea units, including those that occur in earlier sentences. In other words, it is one thing to learn that *if* can be a signal word and another to pay attention to see if *then* is going to pop up soon. But a student who is becoming more fluent, and therefore freeing up more working memory, not only notices if/then but can also manipulate the information on his visual-spatial sketchpad to connect it to the cause-and-effect relationship the author just explained. All that noticing that we speak of in reading instruction is really about getting working memory into the game.

Working memory isn't done with text structure yet. Years of purposeful exposure to text structures, with accompanying modeling, conversation, and application of these signal words in one's own writing, lead to another phase of development. As secondary readers become stronger readers, the number of signal words tends to decline. (If you doubt this, compare a middle school textbook with one in the same content area written for the elementary school market.) The fact is that more sophisticated readers don't need the same number of signal words to describe the same information. Over time, the brain has gotten more efficient at recognizing relationships without so many signal words. Compare these two passages:

> Monarch butterflies migrate annually to Mexico each fall and return when the winter is over. (Flesch-Kincaid Grade Level 10.7)
>
> Monarch butterflies *begin* their migration *south* to Mexico each year in the fall stay for the winter. *After* the winter is over and spring has arrived, they *return* to their homes in the *north*. (Flesch-Kincaid Grade Level 7.7, emphasis added)

The second passage, though longer, is easier to understand, in part, because of the number of signal words featured. *Begin* and *after* serve as sequential signal words, letting the reader know the order in which the events occur. *North* and *south* offer more support, supplying directional information. In the earlier sentence, these concepts must be inferred by the reader. (Note that the Flesch-Kincaid Grade Level measure doesn't directly factor signal words in computing the scores, but rather analyzes the number of syllables, words, and sentences. However, many signal words are short and don't contribute to the difficulty as measured by this readability scale. Multi-syllabic words affect this readability formula greatly.)

You didn't need all that extra support because you have achieved a level of automaticity as it relates to your prior and background knowledge, experience with texts, and ability to direct your attention. In fact, you not only read the first sentence and got it, you were able to conserve your working memory to do a much more difficult task—to compare and analyze the two passages through the lens of a reading expert.

We've spent several pages explaining what working memory is and why it is critical to reading, but as teachers, what we really want to know is, How can I get it into their long-term memory? At the very least, long-enough term memory so they can pass the test? Psychologists Anders Ericsson and Walter Kintsch have been asking the very same thing.

Facilitating Long-Term Memory

Ericsson and Kintsch weren't satisfied with the explanation of working memory, at least when it came to reading. They noted that when people read, they can keep more than seven ideas in their head at the same time (recall the research on digit span). And they were concerned that there was something of a "bright line" drawn between working memory and long-term memory, perhaps falsely suggesting they were two completely separate entities. After all, it's not like there is a wall in your brain separating the two, and if you could get the information from working memory over that wall, then you'd remember it forever. Instead, they proposed that it's a bit more porous and that effective readers utilize a **long-term working memory** (LTWM; Ericsson & Kintsch, 1995).

Here's where it gets very interesting. In studies they have conducted on experts in a variety of fields (violin, chess, even darts), they have noted that what these experts are able to do is access knowledge efficiently when it is needed. Whether it is recognizing chess moves or lining up for a throw of the dart, they can summon up what they know with relatively little effort, saving their working memory for the immediate stuff. In other words, they have a LTWM, a storage place of sorts, where they can readily retrieve what they need.

Remember the analogy of the 13-year-old's closet from Chapter 3? According to Ericsson and Kintsch (1995), one of the reasons that the teenager can't find his metaphorical soccer shoes is because he doesn't have a handy, readily accessible storage place, such as an equipment bag, to get the stuff he uses more frequently. To continue with the analogy, if he was really good at this, he would keep that equipment bag right near the front of the closet so he can grab it at a moment's notice. They go on to say the following:

Thus, LTWM is an expert skill. There are, however, tasks at which most adults in our society are experts. Text comprehension is an example. As long as the texts to be comprehended are simple, reasonably well written, and about familiar, everyday topics, we are all experts. The reading (or listening) skills are practiced over a lifetime.... Thus, we comprehend such texts readily, retrieve relevant knowledge or personal experiences automatically without special effort, and remember what we read, also without special effort. The LTWM mechanism is behind this achievement, and explains why our memory is so good here, and so poor when we read something in an unfamiliar domain. (p. 189)

To state it another way, how we move knowledge of strategies from working memory (where we have to focus a lot of conscious attention) to long-term memory is through repetition. All those opportunities allow the brain to create a LTWM of knowledge that's going to be used a lot—the equivalent of moving some items to the front of the closet where they can be quickly retrieved. So the advice on how to get students to remember what they have been taught is the same advice given to the musician who wanted to know how to get to Carnegie Hall—practice, kid, practice.

This reminds us that students aren't going to learn how to activate strategic moves in their reading through a few exposures. They need the modeling of an expert (who has a long-term working memory to draw upon) to demonstrate how to use text structure to understand the relationships between and among concepts.

Modeling the Use of Text Structure

Informational Text Structures

Informational texts are commonly organized into compare/contrast, problem/solution, cause/effect, chronological/sequence, and descriptive. The way that readers identify the inherent text structure is through the use of signal words. Table 8 contains a list of text structures and common signal words. It is important to note that the goal of modeling text structures is not to have students name the structure used by the author. We don't think it's particularly helpful to give students selections of texts and have them name the structure. Instead, understanding text structure facilitates understanding by reducing the demands on working memory.

For example, during a shared reading of an excerpt of *The Prince* by Niccolo Machiavelli (1908), history teacher Mr. Cooper noted the text structure as a way to organize information. In his words, "I think

Table 8 Common Informational Text Structures and Signal Words

Text Structure	Definition	Signal Words
Compare/ Contrast	A text that describes the similarities and differences between two or more things, places, events, ideas, and so on	although, as well as, as opposed to, both, but, by contrast, compared with, different from, either...or, even though, however, in common, in comparison, instead of, like, on the other hand, otherwise, similar to, similarly, still, unlike, whereas, yet
Problem/ Solution	A text that identifies an issue and how the issue is solved; often the solution becomes another problem	because, consequently, despite, dilemma is, if...then, problem is, puzzle is solved, question/ answer, resolved, result, so that, thus
Cause/Effect	A text that explains how or why something happened	accordingly, as a result of, because, begins with, consequently, effects of, for this reason, if...then, in order to, is caused by, leads/led to, may be due to, so that, steps involved, thereby, therefore, thus, when... then
Chronological/ Sequence/ Temporal	This text presents information in order of time, sequence, or as a process	additionally, after, afterward, another, as soon as, before, during, finally, first, following, immediately, initially, last, later, meanwhile, next, not long after, now, on (date), preceding, second, soon, then, third, today, tomorrow, until, when, yesterday
Descriptive	This text provides details that could be a list or outline	above, across, along, appears to be, as in, behind, below, beside, between, down, for example, for instance, in back of, in addition, in front of, in particular, looks like, near, on top of, onto, outside, over, specifically, such as, to the right/ left, under

that Machiavelli is comparing and contrasting here. I'm thinking that he wants me to understand the difference in the two types of fighting he discusses. I see here, where he says 'You should consider then, that there are two ways of fighting, one with laws and the other with force.' I think he's setting up to compare and contrast these two ways. This leads me to organize my thinking into categories that I can use to help me remember what Machiavelli believes."

Ms. Robinson, a life science teacher, also noted the author's use of text structure while reading about circulating blood. As she said, "So I'm seeing this as a process that occurs in a specific sequence. It reminds me of the water cycle we learned about and how that is also a process. So the author tells me about this in order. I understand from the text structure that blood circulates through the heart chambers, lungs, body and then back again. I see that he's going to describe how carbon dioxide and oxygen are exchanged in the lungs and tissues and I bet that will be a process as well. This whole section is about the processes used by living things. Now that I know it will be a process, I'll get my notes ready so that I can record the major steps of the process."

Narrative Text Structures

Narrative texts also have a common structure; they use story grammar (setting, plot, characters, conflict, etc.) and literary devices to signal readers. When children are first exposed to narrative texts, they learn that stories have a beginning, middle, and end. They also learn to tell the difference between fact and fiction. Some struggling middle and high school students also need modeling on these topics if they have yet to develop this level of understanding. Most middle and high school students, however, are ready for much more complex analyses of literacy. Table 9 contains a list of narrative text structures related to story grammar and exposition with examples from the book *Animal Farm* (Orwell, 1946).

In addition to story grammar, to understand the narrative structure used in fiction, students must acquire a keen sense of the literary devices that authors use as they write. All authors use literary devices to describe, compare, and teach. It is the expert use of literary devices that makes some writing truly artistic. It should be noted that many literary devices are used in informational text as well; however, they are frequently taught first using narrative text structures. Table 10 contains a number of common literary devices presented in alphabetical order. There are of course many other literary devices that authors use to weave their stories.

Table 9 Narrative Text Structure Based on Story Grammar

Element	Definition	Example From *Animal Farm* (Orwell, 1946)
Setting	The physical location used to tell the story	Manor Farm, England, which represents a place that might have existed or could exist today
Point of View	The perspective from which the story is told (first person, third person, omniscient)	3rd person omniscient, which helps the reader understand the perspective of all of the characters at the same time
Plot	The sequence of events, especially how the characters interact with the setting through dialogue	• The farmer doesn't feed the animals so they plan a rebellion • Over time, the oppressed become the oppressors
Characters— Antagonist	A character or group of characters who represent the opposition against which the hero(es) or protagonist(s) must contend	• In the beginning, all of the animals • Over time, some of the animals become protagonists
Characters— Protagonist	The leading character, but not always a hero, typically the protagonist changes or evolves during the story	In the beginning, the three farmers As the novel progresses, the pigs, especially Napoleon
Dialogue	The language that the characters use to convey their ideas and feelings	Example lines of dialogue that have had a lasting effect: • "four legs good, two legs bad" • "some pigs are more equal than others"
Rising Action	A series of events that lead to the climax of the story; action typically relates to the conflicts or struggles of the protagonist	• The animals write their 7 commandments • Animals work hard and have a great harvest • Animals defeat the humans a second time • The farm is divided between Napoleon and Snowball

(continued)

Table 9 Narrative Text Structure Based on Story Grammar *(continued)*

Element	Definition	Example From *Animal Farm* (Orwell, 1946)
Climax	The point of greatest tension and the turning point in the action; also signals the change from rising action to falling action	Napoleon kicks Snowball out of the barn and assumes control of the entire farm
Conflict	The struggle between the opposing forces of which there are five basic forms: person versus person, person versus self, person versus nature, person versus society, and person versus God	• Animals versus Mr. Jones—they want rights for the farm • Snowball versus Napoleon who each wants to lead • Animals versus nature—the windmill is destroyed and the animals have to work with little to eat
Falling Action	The events that follow the climax and end in the resolution	• Napoleon ends meetings, the commandments are changed. Napoleon blames Snowball for everything. • Executions take place. • Animal farm is returned to a republic
Resolution	The point in the story where the conflict has been settled or worked out	Pigs are equal to men

In her shared reading of *Shiloh* (Naylor, 1991), Ms. Brown paused and said, "I see our character changing. Marty has lied before, and he's lying again. But the difference is he knows it. I think that when he realizes this, he's changing. Here's what he says, let me read it again: 'Funny how one lie leads to another and before you know it, your whole life can be a lie' [p. 60]. I think Marty realizes that his whole life could change and that he'll think about this before he lies again.

Similarly, Ms. Ramirez noticed a plot twist in the book *Esperanza Rising* (Ryan, 2000) and shared her thinking with students. In her words, "Now here's a plot twist. Esperanza could see a body in the back of a wagon, and Miguel has his head down and he's crying. I think that this is

Table 10 Common Literary Devices

Term	Definition	Example
Allegory	Story used to teach something, usually long and requiring analysis to find the intention	• The parables in the Bible • Aesop's fables
Alliteration	Occurs when the author uses the same letter or sound to start each word in a string; used frequently in books for emergent readers in part to foster phonemic awareness	*Andrea anxiously awaited arrangement.*
Allusion	Reference to a well-known person, myth, historical event, biblical story	• *She's just like Narcissus.* • *It's as bad as the sinking of the Titanic.*
Flashback	Pauses the action to comment or portray a scene that took place earlier in order to provide more detail about the present character, setting, or plot	During a scene in which a person walks through a dark alley, the author pauses to relate a story about another time the character was scared
Foreshadowing	Hint of things to come—usually, but not always, an unpleasant event	In the beginning of *Where the Red Fern Grows*, there is a dog fight that hints of things to come in the book
Hyperbole	Exaggerated comment or line used for effect and not meant to be taken literally	*When faced with a long line at the Department of Motor Vehicles, Andrew said, "It will take an eternity to be allowed to drive."*
Imagery	Involves language that evokes one or all of the five senses: seeing, hearing, tasting, smelling, touching	• *Her lips taste of honey and dew.* • *Walking through the halls, amid the crashing sound of lockers closing and the smell of yesterday's coffee, I saw the radiant teacher.*

(continued)

Table 10 Common Literary Devices *(continued)*

Term	Definition	Example
Irony	Uses sophisticated humor in relaying a message, often saying what something is when the opposite or reverse could be true; authors use irony to say one thing when they mean another	*James looks at the shark bite out of his surfboard and says, "Great! Now I finally have the short board I always wanted."*
Metaphor	Comparison in which one thing is said to be another; in contrast with similes, metaphors make a direct statement and do not use "like" or "as" to make the comparison.	*The dog's fur was electric, standing on end in fear.*
Personification	Animals, ideas, or actions possess the qualities of humans	*Hate has you trapped in her arms.*
Point of View— First Person	Told from the perspective of the narrator and we readers cannot know or witness anything the narrator does not tell us	*I walked down the dusty lane, listening to the lazy sound of cicadas carried on the warm breeze.*
Point of View— Second Person	The narrator speaks directly to the reader	*You will likely know by now that Andre is a bad guy.*
Point of View— Third Person	Narrator can convey different perspectives at different times and often shifts to different characters' perspectives (third person omniscient or all-knowing), or narrator tells the story as an outsider but from only one person's perspective (third person limited)	*He walked to the store, not looking for anything in particular. Once inside, James waited for a sign.*
Satire	Focuses on mockery or wit to attack or ridicule something; the author considers something to be wrong and uses this literary device to draw the reader's attention to a problem	Mark Twain was a master of satire, as when he wrote, "Reader, suppose you are an idiot. And suppose you were a member of Congress. But I repeat myself." (quoted in Paine, 1912, p. 724)

(continued)

Table 10   Common Literary Devices (continued)

Term	Definition	Example
Simile	Statement in which two things are compared and said to be like or as another	*Like a rain-filled cloud, Anna cried and cried when she learned of her lost fortune.*
Symbolism	Object or action that means something more than its literal meaning	A black crow introduced into the text prepares readers for death; a white dove conveys peace or life.
Tone and Mood	An author presents an attitude and manner of a subject or character as related through dialogue, settings, or descriptions	Hateful, serious, humorous, sarcastic, solemn, objective

Note. Adapted from *Language arts workshop: Purposeful reading and writing instruction* by Nancy Frey and Douglas Fisher. Copyright © 2006 by Nancy Frey and Douglas Fisher. Reprinted with permission from Pearson Education, Upper Saddle River, NJ.

a really important change in the plot. I think so because all of the main characters we've met are there, and I notice that the mood has changed. The author isn't using such happy words any more. I'm thinking that there is something bad about to happen, worse than the death. I know that authors often provide readers hints—foreshadowing—about future events or twists in the plot."

Graphic Organizers Based on Text Structure

Graphic organizers help students visually organize information to support their comprehension. Graphic organizers are useful because they highlight the important ideas in a text and how these ideas are related to one another. They are visual representations of a student's knowledge and are structured to show relationships through labels. Graphic organizers present information in concise ways to show key parts of the whole concept, theme, or topic and are highly effective for all students.

As we noted in Chapter 3, being actively engaged in processing the text supports comprehension. When students are actively engaged, they are using skills such as analyzing, synthesizing, evaluating and summarizing. Graphic organizers help students with these skills by organizing information to show how it is related. As such, a graphic organizer is a tool students can use to reduce the demand on their working memory and facilitate information transfer into long-term memory. Alvermann and Boothby (1982) found that when students used a graphic organizer they became more active readers. When graphic organizers correspond with a specific text structure, they help students clarify connections and relationships between concepts and ideas found in their reading (Fisher & Frey, 2008b). Table 11 contains a sampling of graphic organizers based on specific text structures.

In terms of modeling, it is important to remember that students need examples of the type of thinking required of a task before being asked to complete the task with peers or independently. Accordingly, Mr. Jones modeled the use of a process chart to keep track of the information in a text he was reading. The text presented information about the chain of infection as a process and provided the reader with significant details about how to break each link in the chain. Mr. Jones said to his students, "I skimmed this text and figured out that the author was going to explain a series of events that can lead to infection so I decided to use a chart that would allow me to capture information as I read." As he read, Mr. Jones added information to the process chart, modeling his thinking along the way. For example, when he got to the "portal of exit," Mr. Jones said, "The important point here is that this is the exit plan—the way that the pathogen gets out of an infected host, for example. I don't have a lot of space on my chart, but I don't need it. I only need to take a few notes to help me remember this information."

Mr. Jones knows that he can't (and shouldn't) stop at this point. Too often, he has seen his colleagues treat graphic organizers as the end goal of a lesson rather than an intermediate step to something else. "If all they do is fill out a graphic organizer, then it's no better than a worksheet," he said. "I want them to do something with the information. Sometimes I have them use it to support their discussion, and at other times I'll ask them to write using the graphic organizer. Today, I'm going to have them work in pairs to explain a chain of infection using a scenario I'll give them. They will have their graphic organizers with them so they can support their explanation using the correct academic vocabulary."

Keep This in Mind

Text structures are used by writers to illustrate relationships among concepts, such as comparing and contrasting two phenomena or demonstrating the causes and effects of an event. Often these are

Table 11 Sample Graphic Organizers Based on Text Structure

Text Structure	Type	Description	Example
Compare / Contrast	Venn diagram	Overlapping circles that illustrate similarities and differences between two concepts	
Compare / Contrast	Chart or matrix	Rows and columns in table format that shows relationships vertically and horizontally	
Compare / Contrast	Cause–effect pattern	Based on a central idea, the two sides demonstrate the differences between the two topics	
Problem / Solution	Problem-solution flowchart	The flow from topic to problem to possible solutions to outcome are displayed on this tool	
Cause / Effect	Fishbone map	Based on a line that demonstrates the effect, a number of causes can be identified	

(continued)

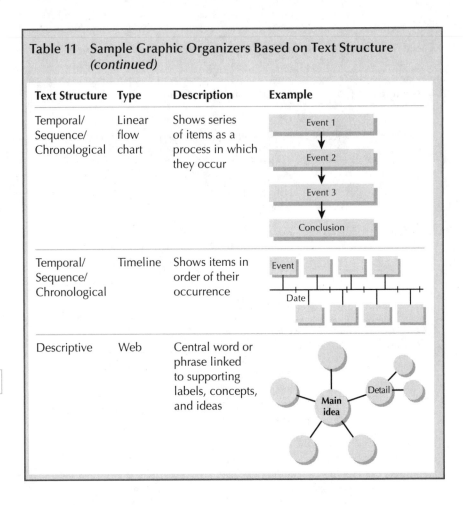

Table 11   Sample Graphic Organizers Based on Text Structure *(continued)*

Text Structure	Type	Description	Example
Temporal/ Sequence/ Chronological	Linear flow chart	Shows series of items as a process in which they occur	Event 1 → Event 2 → Event 3 → Conclusion
Temporal/ Sequence/ Chronological	Timeline	Shows items in order of their occurrence	Event / Date
Descriptive	Web	Central word or phrase linked to supporting labels, concepts, and ideas	Main idea / Detail

accompanied by signal words that serve as guideposts, alerting the reader to a conceptual relationship. In addition, narrative writers use predictable structures to tell their tales. When understood, text structures and signal words help readers make sense of texts. They do so, in part, by freeing working memory so that the reader focuses on comprehension.

What we don't want to see is students filling out worksheets on text structures. Unfortunately, we've been in classrooms in which students were filling out papers ("shut up sheets," as one of our colleagues calls them) focused on naming the structure of a paragraph—nothing more, just naming the structure. This isn't our goal. Our goal is not to have students simply name a text structure and circle signal words. Students need to learn to *use* the structures and signal words as a memory tool and as a study guide. And most important, modeling the use of text structures should be part of an integrated and intentional plan to teach reading for meaning. As we noted in Chapter 3 on comprehension, text structures and signal words can't be taught in a four-week unit once a year. It's got to be part of the ongoing conversation teachers and students have about the things they read.

CHAPTER 6

Text Features: Visual and Linguistics Guidepost

ow do you give driving directions to someone who is lost? Do you provide verbal instructions, such as "Turn left onto 163 North"? Perhaps you add some gestures, motioning with your hands. You might even sketch a simple map. If you're on the receiving end of these directions, you probably appreciate getting the information in as many ways as possible. The words help, of course, but so do the gestures and body position, as well as the visual information. Your brain is busy at work processing the information using all of these modalities—verbal, visual, and kinesthetic. The same is true when reading a text that offers visual information along with the written words. Your reading brain draws upon the words and images offered and it consolidates them into knowledge.

The strategies you use to assist a lost traveler are analogous to the devices used by authors to give direction to a reader. The headings, bolded words, diagrams, and so on are comparable to signposts. Like road signs, they notify readers of what lies ahead and encourage them to pay attention to critical information. However, these guides are useful only to the extent that readers can understand them and then execute the correct maneuver. Like driving, reading requires that consolidation of multiple sources of information that result in well-executed reading maneuvers.

In this chapter, we extend our conversation on the use of nonverbal representations of information, particularly visual ones. We discuss how text features can be incorporated into modeled instruction through think-alouds. But first, we begin by discussing text features and nonverbal representations and how these elements support reading comprehension.

Text Features

We define text features as design elements used in a text to provide a structure to the reading. These features include titles, headings, charts, and photographs. Herman, Anderson, Pearson, and Nagy (1987) described elements such as titles as part of the "macrostructure" and stated that "knowledgeable readers may use such information to gain an initial understanding of the information of the text" (p. 266). Their study of over 400 eighth graders found that revised texts that included items such as titles resulted in increased comprehension, and that these were especially useful when the text was conceptually ambiguous.

More recently, Surber and Schroeder (2007) designed an ingenious study of the effects of headings on the reading comprehension of college students. They gave students a 3,000-word informational passage on a computer that either included headings or did not and assessed them for recall, rereading, and time spent on the passage. They further analyzed the results for students who had high levels of prior knowledge or low levels of prior knowledge. They discovered that both high- and low-prior-knowledge readers who read the passage with headings recalled more information, spent more time on the key information, and read longer than the readers who had to read texts without the headings (Surber & Schroeder, 2007). In addition, these researchers reported that the headings were more useful for readers with high prior knowledge, suggesting that these organizing features complement the learner's understanding of the conceptual structure of the information.

Other text features that further organize longer texts include conventional book elements such as a table of contents, chapters, page numbers, and indexes. These are guideposts in the truest sense because they allow the reader to locate information quickly without getting lost in a sea of words. While these may seem obvious to secondary readers (and therefore not necessary for modeling), in our practice we have found that students, even stronger readers, are much less able to use these than might be assumed. Our conversations have led us to the conclusion that while they received instruction on these organizational elements in elementary school, they have had relatively few opportunities to use them in practice. Think how often you have directed your students to a section of the book without ever allowing them to locate information themselves.

Educational researchers have further broadened the definition of text features to include graphic and typographical design elements such as color, illustrations, diagrams, boldfaced or italicized words, and fonts. We need look no further than our own textbooks to see the evidence of our increasingly visual society. The rise of moving images in the twentieth century has given way to Web-based digital information, and the students we teach today have never known a world where information wasn't displayed on a screen. With each round of textbook adoption it seems that the pages of our textbooks become more crowded with images, colors, and special features. These elements serve to explain, elaborate, illustrate, and notify the reader of important information, but they can also create quite a bit of visual confusion. In particular, readers who struggle can find it difficult to prioritize information and make a plan for reading. As with other text features discussed, they are prime candidates for instructional modeling. A table of the kinds of text features common to secondary textbooks appears in Table 12.

Text features range from those that are text-based, such as titles and headings, to those that are more visual in nature, such as photos, illustrations, and diagrams. These nonverbal representations of information can be more challenging for teachers to model because they draw upon knowledge they may be less accustomed to using during instruction. Yet they can be as informative as the words printed on the page.

Table 12   Common Text Features in Secondary Textbooks

Type of Element	Text Features
Elements That Organize	• Chapters • Titles • Headings • Subheadings • List of figures
Elements for Locating Information	• Table of contents • Indexes • Page numbers
Elements for Explanation and Elaboration	• Diagrams • Charts and tables • Graphs • Glossary
Elements That Illustrate	• Photographs • Illustrations
Elements That Notify	• Bolded words • Italics and other changes in font

Nonverbal Representations

When we invite students to visualize a setting an author describes, draw a figure to represent a process, or use strong imagery in their writing, we are tapping into the learner's nonverbal representations of the world. We know that the brain filters and sorts out literally hundreds of sensory inputs each moment, making determinations about what is unnecessary to consciously attend to (the pressure of your clothes on your skin) and what is vital (the smoke detector going off). Each learner stores these sensory inputs—sounds and physical movement, images and chemical sense perceptions like smell and taste, emotional responses linked to experiences—and can summon these memories for future comparative use.

Dual code theory (DCT), as articulated by Sadoski, Paivio, and Goetz (1991), proposes that reading comprehension occurs through an interaction between two separate sources, or codes, of information. One is a nonlinguistic code (nonverbal) for understanding objects and events and is linked to sensorimotor input such as eye movement and touch, while the other is a linguistic code (verbal) for representing language. The authors theorize that "the text [is] mentally represented in two codes and in at least two different modalities: (1) an audio-motor representation probably experienced as inner speech, and (2) a visuo-spatial representation probably experienced as mental imagery" (Sadoski & Paivio, 2004, p. 1339). They go on to point out that comprehension occurs as an interaction between these two modalities and that in the more skilled reader, these associations are fluent and require less "random-search activation," resulting in a "mental model" that can be readily accessed (Sadoski & Paivio, 2004, p. 1339).

These authors offer a wonderful illustration of DCT in action. They note that when we read *baseball bat*, we process it verbally, ruling out nocturnal animals that fly and differentiating it from the small white object that is struck by the bat. In addition, we draw on sensory experiences such as the feel of it in our hands and the crack of a bat as it makes contact with the ball. Our visual memory of baseball bats is activated as well—is it white ash with a Louisville Slugger oval burned into the barrel? Perhaps it is an aluminum bat, cool to the touch and sporting a matte finish to reduce the reflected glare of the sun. As readers read *baseball bat*, they draw on their prior knowledge and their sensory memories to imbue the term with information beyond the definitional level.

While not all text features tap directly into visual and nonverbal sources of knowledge, many do. The choice of the right photograph can bring a history reading to life—it is hard to imagine a written description of the crash of the German zeppelin Hindenburg without an accompanying still from the historic newsreel footage. Many teachers also play the unforgettable radio coverage by reporter Herbert Morrison as he wailed, "Oh, the humanity..." as the burning airship crashed near spectators gathered to watch the landing. The audio and visual information to be gained transcends the written passage and assists the learner in formulating an understanding of the events of that day.

Some of these can cross over into the realm of graphic organizers (see Chapter 5 for more information). Completed graphic organizers are frequently used in textbooks as a text feature to assist the reader in understanding the concepts in the text. McCrudden, Schraw, Lehman, and Poliquin (2007) studied the comprehension of science students using a diagram that illustrated the causal relationships described in a passage about space travel. Their findings indicate that the use of this visual display of information increased the readers' comprehension. While they provided their test subjects with written directions, we noticed that these directions could easily be modified for use as a think-aloud in modeling by changing the point of view from second person to first person: "This diagram helps me understand information in the text about the effects that the lack of gravity in space have on astronauts. The diagram flows from left to right, starting with 'Lack of Gravity.' The most important effects are indicated by bold arrows and are italicized. When I study the diagram, I pay special attention to the events that lead to the different effects, and also to the order they occur" (original directions can be found in McCrudden, Schraw, Lehman, & Poliquin, 2007, pp. 386–387). A copy of this diagram can be seen in Figure 11.

Modeling the Use of Text Features
Activating Background Knowledge

One of the most useful ways to model the use of certain text features is to show your students how you activate your own background knowledge and plan your reading. Text features that organize the reading and illustrate topics are ideal for this work. Family and consumer sciences teacher Ms. Chapman distributed full color laminated recipe cards to her students to model the way she activated her background knowledge when she read them and said, "I came across this menu for

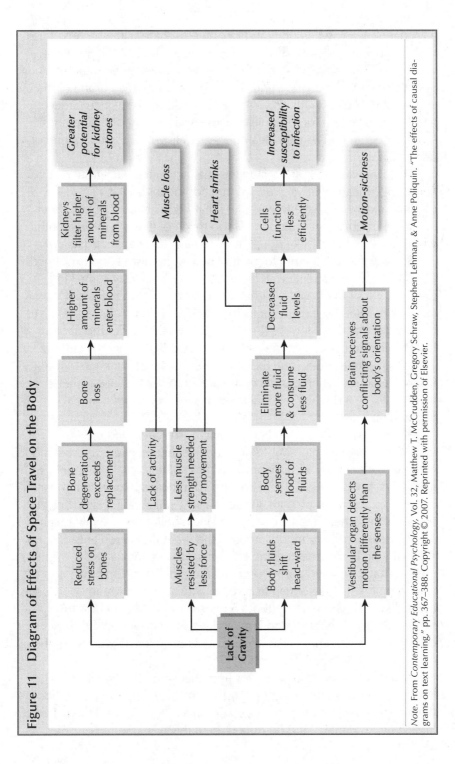

Figure 11   Diagram of Effects of Space Travel on the Body

Note. From *Contemporary Educational Psychology*, Vol. 32, Matthew T. McCrudden, Gregory Schraw, Stephen Lehman, & Anne Poliquin. "The effects of causal diagrams on text learning," pp. 367–388. Copyright © 2007. Reprinted with permission of Elsevier.

a Mediterranean-style dinner and I wanted to share with you how I use what I know to understand what I am reading. The first thing I see, of course, is the word *Mediterranean* in the title. Right away I start thinking about that part of the world and what I know about the cuisine of the region. Lots of olives—that's something I could expect, since Greece and Italy are known for their olive crops. And because they are on the sea, I expect to find fish and seafood. After all, you eat what's plentiful and available."

She also wanted to show students that activating background knowledge means that you rule information out as well. "It's Mediterranean, so I have to consider what I don't expect to find. Beef would be a surprise—you don't get too much of that in this area of the world because there isn't enough land to have large animals like cows."

She pointed out the photograph of one of the dishes and exclaimed, "That sure gets my attention! It looks like a pasta salad of some kind. Can't tell if it's hot or cold—I'll need to read more closely for that information. But it definitely looks Mediterranean to me. I can see olives and peppers, and as I look at the name of the salad under the photo, I can't help but notice that the feta is in it, too: 'Bell Pepper-Feta Pasta Toss.' That sounds great, and the photo tells me it will look great, too. Cooks like to see a photograph of the prepared dish because it helps them visualize it on their own table, and gives them a reference when preparing it."

She continued to model her thinking as she reviewed the list of ingredients, then pointed out to her students that there are a few symbols in the top left corner. "This recipe card has some icons, or symbols, on it. The first one is a clock face showing 30 minutes. I know that means it is a quick recipe to prepare. There is also a single dollar sign. I can't be sure until I check the legend, but a single dollar sign usually means it's inexpensive; the more dollar signs, the more the ingredients cost. The last icon is of some vegetables. That probably means it is a meatless recipe. That'd be good for my vegetarian guests." Ms. Chapman was able to model the use of text features to activate background knowledge by thinking like an expert. Although her students didn't necessarily possess the same background knowledge as her, they could observe how she drew on different sources of knowledge to make sense of the recipe cards.

Text features are also useful for using background knowledge to plan closer reading through skimming and scanning. Arguing that skimming and scanning occur together, Burke (2004) called them 1 of 10 "academic essentials" and described them this way:

Skimming is perfect when you need to cover material you do not need to understand at deeper levels; for example, flipping through an article to determine if it is appropriate for your paper on Cesar Chavez. Scanning, on the other hand, is not so much about reading information as it is about finding it within a text. We scan the movie section to find the time and location of a movie. (p. 51)

British literature teacher Ms. Adams modeled the use of text features from skimming and scanning using a website called "Mr. William Shakespeare and the Internet" sponsored by Palomar College in San Marcos, California (shakespeare.palomar.edu). Her students would soon be writing a research paper on a British author of their choice, and Ms. Adams wanted to model how she locates information on a webpage. Using a data projector to display the information so all could see, she took them to the home page and said, "When I look at an information-rich site like this, the first thing I do is take a look at the site menu on the left side. These buttons give me a great sense of what I could find here. Some of the major topics are 'Works,' 'Life and Times,' and 'Theatre.' Those are similar to the major headings I would find in a print resource. I'm skimming to decide whether I need to spend any more time at this site."

Ms. Adams directed a laser pointer to the screen and pointed out two items. "Look at these two—'Study Guides' and 'Attributions.' What I'm looking at are two terms that are indented under the Works heading, and they're in smaller font, too. They're like subheadings in a book. They are directly related to his works, but get their own categories." She clicked on "Study Guides" to reveal a list of links to individual plays, then returns to "Attributions."

"Hold on, here's something! I wasn't sure what was meant by this term, so I figured I'd better take a look at it so I'd know whether to return to it later or rule it out. As I scanned the first sentence to find specific information on what *attributions* might mean, I saw this: 'This page contains links to plays attributed to Shakespeare, some with more justice than others, but not officially accepted into the canon.' I appreciate that they are very clear on stating that the information about these plays doesn't have the same level of rigor. If I decide to write about disputed plays of Shakespeare, this will be a good place for me to look."

Locating Information in a Text

While most teachers know that readers do not have to read every text from cover to cover, many students do not. Too often, students approach texts thinking that they have to start on the first page and read through until they find the information they're looking for. While this is changing with the increased use of electronic texts, many students still read from the first word to the last word when faced with a printed text.

Most texts have a number of features designed to help readers find information. These features include the table of contents, page numbers, indexes, glossaries, and specialized lists such as figures or primary source documents. Of course, this assumes that readers know what they're looking for. Both of these behaviors—knowing what you're looking for and using text features to locate information—can be modeled by teachers.

For example, mathematics teacher Ms. Scott demonstrated her ability to locate information about intercepts while solving problems related to linear graphs. Ms. Scott looked through the table of contents from several books and found the word she was looking for. In her words, "I want to be sure that I have the right information in my mind about intercepts before I try to complete this linear graph. This book doesn't have anything specifically listed about intercepts, but it does have linear graphs. I think I'll try a different book. [Picking up a second book] This book has a whole section on intercepts. I'll turn to this page and do a quick review before I start solving the problem."

Similarly, Mr. Davies wanted to locate information about resting heart rate for his student athletes. Pointing to the section of resource books in the weight room, he said, "I know that one of those books will have the information I'm looking for. I don't have time to read them all over again; I can use the index to quickly find the information I want. [Flipping through a book] This title, *Fitness Planning*, looks like a good choice. Yep, there it is in the index, resting heart rate. Oh, and look, they give me a table based on age for the target rate. It's so easy to find information when you know what you're looking for and how to find it."

These two examples highlight the ability of teachers to regularly model locating information in texts. In both cases, the teacher knew what he or she was looking for and how to find it. Teachers can also model finding information in response to an essential question or personal quest.

Ms. Hucks, a social studies teacher who is fascinated by Franklin Delano Roosevelt (FDR), regularly models looking at new books for any tidbits about her idol. She also encourages students to be on the lookout for information about their selected historical figure as they read widely in history. On one occasion, Ms. Hucks reviewed her mail in front of the class. She had received a new history magazine and said, "This comes every month, and I always skim the table of contents to see if anyone has anything to say about FDR. I might read some of the other articles, but if there is anything about FDR, I make sure to read it right away. Let's see...Genghis Kahn, Galapagos Islands, President Truman, Phillip the Great.... Nope, nothing on FDR. Well, there's good information in here, but you can't always be lucky enough to find information that you want quickly. I'll keep looking. I'm sure that something will come my way this month that talks about my personal favorite."

Interpreting Graphs, Charts, and Tables

Authors also present information through graphs, charts, and tables, and these text features typically have a great deal of information and are open to a number of interpretations. Interpreting graphs, charts, and tables is not simply a school task; it's something that people do nearly every day. Information presented in graph or chart form is often critical to understanding the text. It's not an extra added for visual stimulation. Interestingly, test makers often require that students interpret information found in graphs, charts, and tables if students are to be scored as proficient.

Types of graphs or charts. In general, graphs and charts come in four basic types: pie charts, bar graphs, line graphs, and XY-plots (or scatterplot). Pie charts show the relationship of parts to a whole and help readers visualize the relationships between related items. For example, the pie chart in Figure 12(a) demonstrates the music preferences for a group of high school students we know. The majority of students sampled preferred rap, as can be seen in the chart. This chart also demonstrates the relative preferences for the remaining 50% of the students.

Bar graphs and line graphs compare values in a category or between categories. They are especially useful for demonstrating the relationship between different variables. For example, the bar graph in Figure 12(b) shows our students' reading habits by day of the week. This includes assigned as well as voluntary reading and is self-reported data. Similarly, an XY-plot also demonstrates a mathematical relationship between two variables.

Types of tables. In general, tables are matrices of information presented in rows and columns. These can be fairly simple, as in a table containing a date and a book read. They can also be fairly complex with lots of columns and rows, demonstrating complex information

Figure 12 Sample Charts

(a) Sample Pie Chart: Music Preferences

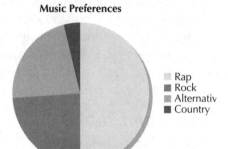

Music Preferences

- Rap
- Rock
- Alternativ
- Country

(b) Sample Bar Graph: Average Number of Minutes Reading at Home

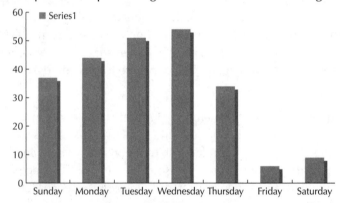

(c) Sample Table: Reading Habits for One High School

Genre	Number of Books per 1000 Students	Average Number of Pages Per Book	Highest Number of Times Any One Book Checked Out	Average Reading Level From a Sample 100-Word Passage
Biography	64	214	39	8.5
General Fiction	280	311	14	11.2
Young Adult Literature	413	139	72	5.9
Informational	349	277	58	8.2

and relationships. Newspapers are notorious for presenting information in tables as a lot of detail can be included in a small amount of space. Consider the table in Figure 12(c), which presents a great deal of information about the reading habits of a group of high school students. It also demonstrates the types of books they have access to and what they choose to read. There are a number of questions that could be asked of this data, including

- What is the most popular genre in the collection?
- Which genre is read most?
- Which books are most difficult in the collection?
- If you had $100 to spend, what would you buy?

The way students learn to think about information that is presented in graphic, chart, or table format begins with teacher modeling. Students need a number of examples of using these text features and gaining information from these features. For example, earth science teacher Rebecca Jessop showed her students information from the National Oceanic and Atmospheric Administration (NOAA) website (see Figure 13). As she talked, she explained her thinking about the chart: "I see this trend line, and it's not slowing down. I know that this is a positive trend, as I can

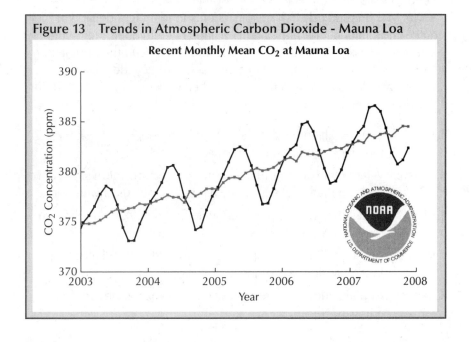

Figure 13   Trends in Atmospheric Carbon Dioxide - Mauna Loa

read the scale on the left side of the chart. The red lines seem to imply that there is an up and down trend within the year. But I notice that each year has four small tick marks—do you see them? I bet that's an indicator for each season: fall, spring, summer, and winter. It makes sense that the carbon dioxide concentration would change during the year, based on the seasons, but I can easily see that the overall trend is increasing concentration. If I were asked a question about the overall trend, I'd know the answer. I'd also be able to discuss the idea that there is a carbon dioxide cycle; times when the concentration is lower or higher than the average for the year. What other trends do you see? Take a minute and construct a question about this graph with your partners, and we'll see if we can use the graph to answer the questions."

While displaying a population growth chart for the years 1900 to 2000, U.S. history teacher Mr. Wilson explained his thinking about the text feature: "This chart shows the rise of population throughout the years. One of the things I notice is that Jefferson was president to fewer than 50,000,000 people. This was probably hard enough, but the President today has to administer a country with over 350,000,000! I also noticed that there are certain decades with much higher growth than others. When I think about the 1920s for example, I see that the population was already over 106 million. In my mind, the 1920s conjures up images of art deco, World War I, which was also known as the war to end all wars, and the Harlem Renaissance."

Mr. Wilson then asked triads of students to identify a decade of their choice and to notice the population change. He reminded them of his example and asked them to make associations between the population changes and what they knew about their selected decade. Javier, Chelsea, and Mario selected the 1960s. Their conversation included the following comments:

Javier: The population was up to 177 million people but that wasn't the biggest jump in U.S. history.

Chelsea: When I think of the 1960s, I think of what my mom says: flower power. I think that's what the hippies of the 60s always said.

Javier: [Laughing] The hippies were wild, but they couldn't dress to save their lives!

Mario: And I think about the protests. They had Martin Luther King, Jr., and Malcolm X trying to get us rights.

Chelsea: And all kinds of protests, too, like Chavez for farmers and anti-war.

The conversation these students had is typical of those that follow teacher modeling. When students are provided examples of the thinking and vocabulary expected of the task, they are able to incorporate the examples into their own behavior. While still apprentices, these students are beginning to see things in the charts and graphs that they might not have noticed before because their teacher taught them how to see the features.

Text Features and Note-Taking

In addition to the comprehension clues that text features provide the reader, text features can be used to guide note-taking efforts. As Skeans (2000) reminded us, readers should engage with texts with a pen in hand. Readers can use their pens (or pencils) to write margin notes or to take notes. We know that reading for understanding means doing something with the text, not simply passing your eyes over it. Without instruction, specifically without modeling from their teachers, students write down or underline random bits of information from the texts they read.

Effectively using a pen while reading requires two things. First, students have to understand the purpose of their reading. Reading the same piece of text with two different purposes will result in different sets of notes. Consider the short text about a house in Figure 14, which was developed by Pichert and Anderson (1977). Reading this piece of text without any particular purpose would likely result in random notes of items of interest. However, as Tovani (2000) noted, reading this text from the perspective of a homebuyer is very different from reading this short story from the perspective of a burglar.

Second, students need to use guideposts as they read as indicators of important ideas for their notes. These guideposts include boldfaced or italicized words, headings, and titles. These guideposts can be incorporated into note-taking as was demonstrated by Ms. Theime in her reading of a *Discover* magazine article about unsolved mysteries of the brain (Eagleman, 2007). As she said to her biology students, "I see that the text is organized with headings for 10 questions and answers. I'll use each of these questions to organize my notes. I don't need to copy the questions exactly, as I have the article. But I will write a main idea in my minor column so that I can add details about the topic as I read the text. I also see that there are a number of quote marks. I'll keep that in mind as I take notes. I predict that the quotes will be helpful in my notes." Ms. Theime began reading the article and taking notes using the guide she had created. Several paragraphs into the text, she read the following:

It is likely that mental information is stored not in single cells but in populations of cells and patterns of their activity. However, it is currently not clear how to know which neurons belong to a particular group; worse still, current technologies (like sticking fine electrodes directly into the brain) are not well suited to measuring several thousand neurons at once. Nor is it simple to monitor the connections of even one neuron: A typical neuron in the cortex receives input from some 10,000 other neurons. (p. 56)

Figure 14   Reading Text With Different Perspectives

The House

The two boys ran until they came to the driveway. "See, I told you today was good for skipping school," said Mark. "Mom is never home on Thursday," he added. Tall hedges hid the house from the road so the pair strolled across the finely landscaped yard. "I never knew your place was so big," said Pete. "Yeah, but it's nicer now than it used to be since Dad had the new stone siding put on and added the fireplace."

There were front and backdoors and a side door which led to the garage which was empty except for three parked 10 speed bikes. They went in the side door, Mark explaining that it was always open in case his younger sisters got home earlier than their mother.

Pete wanted to see the house so Mark started with the living room. It, like the rest of the downstairs, was newly painted. Mark turned on the stereo, the noise of which worried Pete. "Don't worry, the nearest house is a quarter mile away," Mark shouted. Pete felt more comfortable observing that no houses could be seen in any direction beyond the huge yard.

The dining room, with all the china, silver, and cut glass, was no place to play so the boys moved into the kitchen where they made sandwiches. Mark said they wouldn't go to the basement because it had been damp and musty ever since the new plumbing had been installed.

"This is where my Dad keeps his famous paintings and his coin collection," Mark said as they peered into the den. Mark bragged that he could get spending money whenever he needed it since he'd discovered that his Dad kept a lot in the desk drawer.

There were three upstairs bedrooms. Mark showed Pete his mother's closet which was filled with furs and the locked box which held her jewels. His sisters' room was uninteresting except for the color TV which Mark carried to his room. Mark bragged that the bathroom in the hall was his since one had been added to his sisters' room for their use. The big highlight in his room, though, had a leak in the ceiling where the old roof had finally rotted.

Note. From J.W. Pichert, & R.C. Anderson, "Taking different perspectives on a story." *Journal of Educational Psychology, 69,* pp. 309–315. Copyright © 1977 by American Psychological Association (APA). Reprinted with permission.

Following this read-aloud, Ms. Theime added some details to her note-taking guide. If there is any question that modeling transfers to student habits, see the notes of one of her students shown in Figure 15. While reading about DNA, Drew took notes in much the same way

---

Figure 15   Note Page for Biology

Unsolved Brain Mysteries	
Coding Information	Not just one neuron
	Likely information is contained in pathways or patterns of neurons
	Current technology isn't good at measuring more than 1 neuron at a time
Storing Memory	Physical structure changes
	Short-term (like phone number) different from long-term
	Might be in the synapse—the gap between neurons
	Associations—more stable or permanent pathways
	Associations are probably better memory holders
	Memory formation is hard to explain, but memory retrieval is even harder to explain
	*Wow—when you remember something, that memory is easier to erase (they can get blocked an not be restored ... happens because of chemicals).

Summary
Coding information is complex and probably happens along pathways. This creates memories and memories can get erased. Associations are stronger memories.

that his teacher modeled. Of course, Ms. Theime was still modeling her thinking as her students incorporated these behaviors into their habits.

Keep This in Mind

The text features found in textbooks, popular press publications, and on websites are there to organize and guide reading. Others serve to assist the reader in locating information and include indexes and tables of content. Still others explain and elaborate through pictorial representations. Other text features are designed to help readers notice critical information and vocabulary. Text features are sometimes idiosyncratic to the content, such as the graphs in a mathematics text or the organization of a recipe card. In all cases, modeling by the teacher allows students to see how these design elements are purposeful and convey conceptual and content knowledge.

Importantly, text features provide the reader with a different way to think about the content. Printed words, the squiggles found on a page, activate specific neurons in the occipital lobe. Visuals, such as illustrations and pictures, activate different neurons. When visual and textual information are presented together, more neurons fire. This gives the brain more information to sort. When the associations are clear to the reader, the added information increases comprehension. When they're not clear, the brain spends valuable time attempting to make connections. The risk in this situation is that meaning is lost.

As with text structures, modeling and instruction on the uses of text features is useful for supporting reading comprehension. As their readings become denser and their textbooks grow more visually oriented, learners must rely on features and visual representations as never before. There is evidence that reading involves both linguistic and nonlinguistic elements that coalesce in the mind of a skilled reader. However, as with other aspects of comprehension, modeling by an expert reader (the teacher) can help students become stronger readers.

CHAPTER 7

Through Others, We Become Ourselves: Learning With Our Colleagues

A s we noted in Chapters 1 and 2, modeling is an important component in teaching. Of course, the modeling must be followed by opportunities to practice and apply skills. It is also important to note that modeling is not all teacher talk. As has been highlighted by the expert teachers throughout each chapter, modeling provides students with an example of the thinking and academic vocabulary required of the task. Teachers invite students into the conversation, following their thinking.

The DVD included with this book provides an opportunity to see teachers modeling. These video clips may be used as a discussion starter for a group of educators or as a way to provoke thought for the individual viewer. These are real teachers in real classrooms modeling for their students. They should provide you with an opportunity to experience student reactions to modeling and see how much students gain when their teachers model.

Classroom Examples on DVD

Video Clip #1

The first video clip shows a group of students singing the brain song first mentioned in Chapter 2; the song was designed to help you remember the information in that chapter. Linda Lungren included a number of targeted vocabulary words from the chapters of this book in the song. We hope you'll sign along with the students to build your background knowledge and vocabulary so that the information presented in this book is easier to remember.

Video Clip #2

In the second video clip, Kelly Moore models her comprehension using a piece of narrative text. She starts her lesson by activating her students' background knowledge using historic pictures. As she reads, she explains what happens in her mind. Along the way, she purposefully points out tricky words, the background information that is useful to her, and a text feature (footnote) that helps her understand a term. Following her modeling, she asks students to think aloud for their peers using a fishbowl technique. In a fishbowl, a group of students serve as models for a technique while other students observe. This allows the teacher to provide guided instruction as needed, and gives learners an opportunity to clarify their understanding. As you watch the video clip, consider the following questions:

- In what ways does the teacher help students understand the importance of monitoring comprehension?
- How does the teacher use the anticipatory activity to build prior knowledge? Does she draw upon this during the modeling phase of instruction?
- Why do you believe she chose to conduct a think-aloud on the second day, after the students were introduced to the text?
- How does the fishbowl technique support a gradual release of responsibility? How does this relate to your understanding of working memory and rehearsal?

Video Clip #3

In the third video clip, Christine Johnson models the vocabulary and text features necessary for reading and interpreting a map. It is early in the school year, and she emphasizes inclusive participation through choral responses to increase student engagement. The teacher introduces eight vocabulary terms (*title, legend, map index, scale bar, grid, meridian, parallel latitudes,* and *compass rose*) and models her thinking about how she uses and understands these terms. She also provides formal definitional support for learning them. Questions for discussion or reflection include

- What purposes are served by having the students attempt to locate features before modeling?

- How does she incorporate repetition into the lesson to reinforce learning?
- What methods does she use to check for understanding?
- Her modeling focuses on the types of questions she believes her students might ask of themselves. Why do you believe she modeled student questions?

Video Clip #4

John Goodwin demonstrates for his students how to apply vocabulary they have been learning to describe a piece of commercial art. He begins by reviewing target vocabulary and then demonstrates how he uses these terms to describe a logo. His students listen closely to his description and attempt to replicate the image, relying only on his use of terminology. Students then sit back-to-back and work in pairs (also called a barrier game) to replicate a different image using the target vocabulary. He finishes this portion of the lesson by showing two sketches drawn in response to descriptions of the same image and asks his students to identify the elements that were correctly represented. After you watch this video clip, discuss the following questions with colleagues:

- Why do you believe he began the lesson with a review of vocabulary? How does this relate to your understanding of neuronal pathways?
- What are his students able to learn through his demonstration of the use of specific terminology?
- In what ways does motivation and interest play a role in the barrier game activity?
- In terms of comprehension, students are also visualizing. How might this create and reinforce neuronal pathways?

Video Clip #5

In the fifth video clip, Maria Grant thinks aloud as she reads a science text. She consolidates each of the four components we discuss in this book and provides students with examples of comprehension, word solving, text structure, and text features. She also relies on her background knowledge in making meaning. When she finishes with modeling, she provides students with an opportunity to make connections with the text using their own prior experiences. Following the reading, students complete a lab focused on chemical reactions. As you watch the video, look for examples to answer these questions:

- How might the teacher modeling prepare students for their lab experiences?

- It what ways does the teacher model the use of visual representations to activate background knowledge and formulate predictions?

- How does Maria's use of academic language scaffold students' understanding of the text? And how does her use of this language communicate her high expectations for her students?

Video Clip #6

In the sixth video, Aida Allen conducts a shared reading of an informational text with a small group of students. She uses a reciprocal teaching model (Palincsar & Brown, 1986) that highlights the ways in which a reader makes predictions, summarizes information, generates questions, and clarifies confusing information. Her students are early in the reciprocal teaching process and are becoming familiar with the elements, but are not yet ready to use it within a student-led conversation. She moves between modeling and guided instruction as she thinks aloud and then asks students to use their knowledge to become more familiar with the steps while providing prompts, cues, and questions. At the same time, she ensures that students are learning the content of the reading. Use these questions to reflect on this video clip:

- How does the teacher use previous learning about the reciprocal teaching process in this lesson?

- To what extent does she factor text features into her shared reading?

- The teacher mispronounces *turbines* to model a type of confusion learners may have when reading. In what ways does her planned confusion allow her students to take on the role of clarifiers?

- Near the end of the lesson, the teacher shifts to guided instruction by asking a student for evidence of her prediction. How does this support the student's awareness of her own comprehension?

- In what ways do you believe the use of the graphic organizer fosters temporal pooling?

Video Clip #7

Dina Burow reminds us in the final video clip that modeling does not have to come at the beginning of the lesson. She begins with productive group work as students apply recently learned knowledge of graphing functions to solve word problems. She checks for understanding using polling and then models how she interprets the scenarios mathematically using background knowledge. She then asks students to return to their collaborative groups to construct new scenarios using graphs of functions. As you watch the video, look for examples to answer these questions:

- Notice how the teacher integrates her science content knowledge. In what ways do you think interdisciplinary connections build schemata and hierarchical representations?
- How does the teacher provide vocabulary instruction to answer a student's question about the difference between a circle and an ellipse? How does the student then use this knowledge to answer a subsequent problem?
- In what ways has student confidence and competence increased by the end of the lesson?

An Invitation

Throughout this book we have shared our own thinking about modeling through think-alouds and shared reading. In addition, we have incorporated research from fields outside reading, especially biology, cognitive psychology, and neuroscience, to extend our understanding of the role of modeling within a gradual release of responsibility model of instruction. We truly believe that sharing knowledge within and across disciplines can inform our profession and strengthen our practices. We invite you to do the same. We have included in Appendix B an observation tool for examining these practices so that you can engage in collaborative conversations with your colleagues.

We hope this book will inspire you to open up the doors of your classroom to others so that they can provide helpful feedback about your practices, and so that they can learn from you. As well, we encourage you to spend time in the company of other teachers as they instruct students. We have learned so much from spending time in the company of good teachers, some of whom you have met through these video clips. They continually challenge us to expand our understanding of teaching and learning. As Vygotsky (1997) observed, "Through others, we become ourselves" (p. 105). Whether viewed through the developmental psychology lens of the early 20th century, or through the research on mirror neurons of the 21st, modeling is at the root of how we continue to grow as learners.

Modeling Using *Wolf Rider* by Avi (1986)

Introduction

Ask if anyone in the class has heard of this author. Comment about other books has he written. Note the type of books he likes to write.

Note the publication date—1986. What technology did we not have or not commonly use at that time. (It is important to note that caller ID was not commonly used.)

Discuss the idea of crying wolf and what that means. This will allow students to get a sense of the author's play on words for the title as well as allow them to question the events as they occur.

Part 1

p. 3   Andy is a fast thinker—how do I know that? He writes a quick note to his friend to trace the call.

p. 7   The caller says, "I had to punish her." Why? Because she makes fun of people? Think about how we treat other people.

p. 10   The cop says, "Welfare checks just out"—how is the cop stereotyping people? Is that fair? Does he believe the call?

p. 14   Where is Andy's mom? What has happened to her? Prediction opportunity—what clues has the author given you about Andy's family situation?

p. 21   Why doesn't Andy want to go to the cemetery? When you lose someone, how do you get past that? How do you come to terms with the loss of a loved one?

p. 23	His dad is a math teacher—connections to the curriculum? Predict how math might be used in this mystery.
p. 24	Now we know about Andy's mother—killed by a drunk driver. This is an opportunity to discuss drinking and driving. Make a connection to the book previously read aloud last year—*Whirligig*—as there was a drunk driver in that book as well.

Part 2

p. 38	Should Andy tell her she's in trouble? What evidence does he have? Could telling her cause him more trouble?
p. 48	Prediction—why is Andy called in to the counselor's office? Does she believe him or not?
p. 49	Discuss the fable of the boy who cried wolf. How has this story, thus far, differed or been the same as the fable?
p. 69	Dorfman says, "Give me something I can believe." What could Andy provide? What would help people believe him?
p. 71	Is this really happening or is this in Andy's imagination? Discuss posttraumatic stress and how people respond to extremely stressful situations.
p. 82	What had the math secretary done with that note? Make a prediction about the caller and what might happen. Ask students to complete the "I am" poem (see p. 127) based on one of the characters in the book and share with the class.

Part 3

p. 92	Andy wonders if he is wrong. Have you ever doubted yourself? What did you do as a result of that doubt? Do other people doubt you? How can you show them that they are wrong?
p. 97	Discuss the difference between high school and college. The bells don't ring, but what else?
p. 102	What is tenure? Why is tenure important (academic freedom)?
p. 105	Andy's dad says, "You're a very mixed-up young man." What does he mean by that? Does he think that Andy is

crying wolf? Why else does he think that Andy is mixed up (summarize)?

p. 111   Would you send Andy away? Why or why not? What would be the benefit to Andy for taking a vacation as they suggest?

p. 118   The author notes, "It cut across the silence like a muted scream." Think about the specific words that the author has chosen. Why do those words make sense in this story? What images do they create in your mind?

p. 126   It's time to summarize the story so far—make notes about what has happened, what we know, what we want to know. Then, predict what might happen next. Remember that this is about crying wolf and that it's classified under the genre of mystery.

Part 4

p. 135   As the reader, you know that Andy is caught. How does the point of view—first person versus third person—help you understand the story? What will Andy do once he realizes that he's caught?

p. 139   Why is Andy rude to Peggy? Are you ever rude to your parent's friends? Why? What's the point of being rude?

p. 148   "Andy climbed on a wolf." What's the author trying to say here? Why the symbolism? Why is it so obvious?

p. 156   What are Andy's motives now? What are his father's motives? How do these two characters' motives differ?

p. 163   This part ends with Andy saying "wolf." Why? What is he thinking?

p. 163   Ask students to update their "I am" poems based on what they know about their chosen character now.

Part 5

p. 167   Why did Dr. Lucas need to have the irregular sound of someone hard at work? What is he planning to do?

p. 168   What is a cliché? What clichés do you know? Where do they come from? Why does the author focus on the idea of a cliché here?

p. 174   Dr. Lucas decides to act as if Peter Smith is acting alone. What would be the difference if he were acting alone or as part of a group?

p. 176   Why does Andy stop by his old house first? What does that do for him?

p. 193   Why not tell the truth? What does he have to lose now?

p. 202   He drops the cufflink into the trash—wet with tears. What does this mean? What does he know or suspect? What will he do with this information?

"I Am" Poem Template

I am

I wonder

I hear

I want

I am

I pretend

I feel

I touch

I worry

I cry

I am

I understand

I say

I dream

I try

I hope

I am

Think-Aloud Record of Narrative or Informational Text

Think-Aloud Record of Narrative or Informational Text

Teacher _____ Observer _____

Subject _____ Period _____ Date _____

Teacher is modeling how to...	Students are...

Teacher is modeling how to...

1. Figure out…

_____ what the text or
        problem is about.

_____ an unfamiliar word.

Students are…

_____ following along in the text
        as the teacher reads.

_____ taking notes.

_____ conversing with teacher/peers.

_____ off task.

Example of what the teacher should say: (Teacher shows how to figure out unknown word or how to skim text or problem.)

- When I look at this title, I think this is probably _____ because
  _____.
- I'm not sure how to say this word or what it really means.
- When a word is confusing or I don't know it, I….
- It probably sounds like….
- The words around it make me think it might mean….

2. Make or revise predictions…

_____ about the text, problem or story topic based on title, facts, and
        illustrations.

_____ about the characters, events, nonfiction facts.

_____ about what is about to happen.

Example of what the teacher should say: (Teacher makes predictions that will be checked later.)

- I always skim the layout of the text or problem to get an idea about what I'll be reading.
- The title makes me think this is going to be about….
- At first I thought _____, but now I think _____.

3. Make connections…

_____ to other texts or problems.

_____ to prior experiences.

_____ to portions of the same text.

<u>Example of what the teacher should say</u>: (Teacher will connect to a previously read text or experience.)

- Reading this text makes me think….
- Reading this text reminds me of….

4. Ask questions…

_____ about the characters, events, or facts.

_____ about the information that wasn't presented.

<u>Example of what the teacher should say</u>: (Teacher questions character's actions or personality, that is being discussed in text or story or the presentation of the information, graphics, pictures, or problem.)

- I wonder why….

5. Summarize or synthesize…

_____ about the story or character.

_____ about the information.

<u>Example of what the teacher should say</u>: (Teacher summarizes the story or text. Refers back to the title or earlier made predictions about the title or features.)

- Oh, so this is what this was about…

Notes/Suggestions

In a Reading State of Mind: Brain Research, Teacher Modeling, and Comprehension Instruction by Douglas Fisher, Nancy Frey, and Diane Lapp. © 2009 by the International Reading Association. May be copied for classroom use.

Glossary of Neurosciences Terminology

Amygdala: This almond-shaped structure located deep in the brain processes emotional reactions and formulates memories related to emotions.

Angular gyrus: Located in the parietal lobe, it is believed that this structure converts language into the internal dialogue one uses to direct action and thought. More recently, the angular gyrus is also believed to play a role in understanding metaphors. Damage to this area impacts the ability to read, especially in allowing a person to name objects and associate words with other sensory inputs.

Aphasia: This term is used to describe language disorders that interfere with a person's ability to produce or understand language. Aphasia can occur because of a brain injury, stroke, disease, or cognitive disability. The type of aphasia depends on the part of the brain that is injured or damaged.

Arcuate fasciculus: This is a neuronal pathway that connects Broca's area (speech production) to Wernicke's area (comprehension).

Articulatory loop: See *phonological loop*

Association areas: This term refers to the point at which the lobes meet. These areas facilitate complex perceptions related to sensory input, movement, and emotion.

Automaticity: This is the ability to perform a skill unconsciously, often freeing up working memory for other tasks.

Broca's area: Located in the left frontal lobe, this area of the brain regulates speech production and language processing.

Central executive function: A component of a three-part model of working memory, this directs the phonological loop and the visuo-spatial sketchpad that preserves nonlinguistic representations. The central executive function also regulates the flow of information through working memory.

Cerebellum: Called "the small brain," this cauliflower-shaped structure controls and coordinates muscular activity and movement.

Frontal lobe: This is the lobe located at the front of the brain, which performs a major role in language, planning, motivation, and judgment.

Hierarchical representation: This is an information tree, network, or schema of related concepts.

Hippocampus: These two seahorse-shaped limbic system structures, located in the temporal lobes, help to store declarative (factual) and spatial (location) memories.

Long-term working memory: This is a conceptualization of how experts rapidly retrieve knowledge needed to perform a skill. It is thought that experts devote a portion of their working memory to frequently needed skills, such as the coordinated movements needed for a professional golfer's swing.

Mesolimbic pathway: This is a major neuronal pathway associated with dopamine neurotransmitters and responsible for pleasure and addiction.

Midbrain: This term describes the deep structures of the brain that form a pathway for motor functions and produce the neurotransmitter dopamine.

Mirror neurons: This term refers to a network of neurons that fire when a person performs an act or sees someone else perform the same act. Mirror neurons may play an important role in modeling.

Neocortex: Latin for "new bark," these are the outer layers of the brain and contain the gray matter that form the ridges and grooves of the brain.

Neurons: These are specialized cells that transmit nerve impulses electrically across the synapses (spaces) located between nerve cells.

Neuronal pathways: These are organized cellular circuits that fire together. Neuronal pathways are strengthened through repetition and use.

Neuroplasticity: This describes the brain's ability to change due to learning, and to remap itself if damage occurs.

Occipital lobe: This lobe is located at the back of the brain, and it processes and interprets visual information and coordinates with other lobes.

Parietal lobe: This lobe, located near the top of the skull, coordinates and processes movement and spatial knowledge and utilizes information from other lobes, including vision and hearing, to do so.

Phonological loop: Part of a three-part model of working memory, this is the rehearsal loop that preserves a memory for the short-term through repetition of words. Repeating a phone number until it is dialed is an example of activating a phonological loop.

Prefrontal cortex: This portion of the frontal lobe is responsible for decision-making, social behaviors, and personality. Phineas Gage's brain injury significantly damaged the prefrontal cortex and altered his personality and behavior.

Sensory-motor cortex: This is the primary area for coordination of sensory and motor functions, including touch and movement.

Temporal lobe: This refers to the two lobes on both sides of your brain are responsible for auditory perceptions and speech production, and work closely with the occipital lobe (visual).

Temporal pooling: Related to hierarchical representations, this is the cognitive process of gathering details together to form higher conceptualizations and categories. For example, your ability to temporally pool *tabby*, *Siamese*, and *alley* allows you to place these within a larger schema called *cat*.

Visual cortex: This is the area of the brain that controls two important neuronal pathways (the dorsal and ventral streams), allowing readers to see a word and rapidly identify its meaning.

Visual-spatial sketchpad: This is a component of working memory that stores nonlinguistic representations of information, especially visual, sensory, and kinesthetic information.

Wernicke's area: Located in the left temporal lobe, this area controls language comprehension of spoken words.

Working memory: This is a term that replaced short-term memory and is thought to explain how humans temporarily store information and new learning.

Adcock, R.A., Thangavel, A., Whitfield-Gabrieli, S., Knutson, B., & Gabrieli, J.D.E. (2006). Reward-motivated learning: Mesolimbic activation precedes memory formation. *Neuron, 50*(3), 507–517. doi:10.1016/j.neuron.2006.03.036

Afflerbach, P., Pearson, P.D., & Paris, S.G. (2008). Clarifying differences between reading skills and reading strategies. *The Reading Teacher, 61*(5), 364–373. doi:10.1598/RT.61.5.1

Alexander, P.A., Schallert, D.L., & Hare, V.C. (1991). Coming to terms: How researchers in learning and literacy talk about knowledge. *Review of Educational Research, 61*(3), 315–343.

Allington, R.L. (2002). You can't learn much from books you can't read. *Educational Leadership, 60*(3), 16–19.

Alvermann, D.E., & Boothby, P.R. (1982, September). *A strategy for making content reading successful: Grades 4–6.* Paper presented at the annual meeting of the Plains Regional Conference of the International Reading Association, Omaha, NE.

Anders, P.L., & Bos, C.S. (1986). Semantic feature analysis: An interactive strategy for vocabulary development and text comprehension. *Journal of Reading, 29*(7), 610–616.

Armbruster, B.B. (1984). The problem of "inconsiderate text." In G.G. Duffy, L.R. Roehler, & J. Mason (Eds.), *Comprehension instruction: Perspectives and suggestions* (pp. 202–217). New York: Longman.

Armbruster, B.B. (1996). Considerate texts. In D. Lapp, J. Flood, & N. Farnan (Eds.), *Content area reading and learning: Instructional strategies* (pp. 47–58). Boston: Allyn & Bacon.

Baddeley, A.D., & Hitch, G.J. (1974). Working memory. In G.H. Bower (Ed.), *The psychology of learning and motivation* (Vol. 8, pp. 47–90). New York: Academic Press.

Bakken, J.P., & Whedon, C.K. (2002). Teaching text structure to improve reading comprehension. *Intervention in School and Clinic, 37*(4), 229–233. doi:10.1177/105345120203700406

Beck, I.L., McKeown, M.G., Hamilton, R.L., & Kucan, L. (1997). *Questioning the author: An approach for enhancing student engagement with text.* Newark, DE: International Reading Association.

Beck, I.L., McKeown, M.G., & Kucan, L. (2002). *Bring words to life: Robust vocabulary instruction.* New York: Guilford.

Bernstein, B. (1970). Social class, language, and socialization. In P.P. Giglioli (Ed.), *Language and social context: Selected readings* (pp. 157–178). London: Penguin.

Blachowicz, C.L.Z., & Ogle, D. (2001). *Reading comprehension: Strategies for independent learners.* New York: Guilford.

135

Blachowicz, C.L.Z., & Fisher, P. (2000). Vocabulary instruction. In M.L. Kamil, P.B. Mosenthal, P.D. Pearson, & R. Barr (Eds.), *Handbook of reading research* (Vol. 3, pp. 503–523). Mahwah, NJ: Erlbaum.

Block, C.C., Rodgers, L.L., & Johnson, R.B. (2004). *Comprehension process instruction: Creating reading success in grades K–3.* New York: Guilford.

Bloom, B.S. (1986). Automaticity, the hands and feet of genius. *Educational Leadership, 43*(5), 70–77.

Borror, D.J. (1988). *The dictionary of word parts and combining forms.* Mountain View, CA: Mayfield.

Boscolo, P., & Mason, L. (2003). Topic knowledge, text coherence, and interest: How they interact in learning from instructional texts. *Journal of Experimental Education, 71*(2), 126–148.

Burke, J. (2004). "Academic essentials" scaffold success. *Voices From the Middle, 12*(1), 50–51.

California State Board of Education. (2007). Grades 11 & 12 English-language arts content standards. Retrieved June 30, 2008, from www.cde.ca.gov/be/st/ss/enggrades11-12.asp

Calvin, W.H., & Bickerton, D. (2000). *Lingua ex machina: Reconciling Darwin and Chomsky with the human brain.* Cambridge, MA: MIT Press.

Campbell, J.R., Voekl, K.E., & Donahue, P.L. (1997). *NAEP 1996 trends in academic progress* (NCES Publication No. 97–985). Washington, DC: U.S. Department of Education.

Carter, R. (1998). *Mapping the mind.* Berkeley: University of California Press.

Chambliss, M.J. (1994). Evaluating the quality of textbooks for diverse learners. *Remedial and Special Education, 15*(6), 348–362.

Ciardiello, A.V. (2002). Helping adolescents understand cause/effect text structure in social studies. *Social Studies (Maynooth, Ireland), 93*(1), 31–36.

Collins, A., & Smith, E.E. (1980). *Teaching the process of reading comprehension* (Technical Report No. 182). Urbana: University of Illinois, Center for the Study of Reading.

Cunningham, A.E., & Stanovich, K.E. (1998). What reading does for the mind. *American Educator, 22*(1–2), 8–15.

Daniels, H. (2006). What's the next big thing in literature circles? *Voices From the Middle, 13*(4), 10–15.

Dehaene, S., & Cohen, L. (2007). Cultural recycling of cortical maps. *Neuron, 56*(2), 384–398.

Diamond, J.M. (2006). *The third chimpanzee: The evolution and future of the human animal.* New York: Harper Perennial.

Donald, M. (1991). *Origins of the modern mind: Three stages in the evolution of culture and cognition.* Cambridge, MA: Harvard University Press.

Durkin, D. (1979). What classroom observations reveal about reading instruction. *Reading Research Quarterly, 14*(4), 481–533. doi:10.1598/RRQ.14.4.2

Eagleman, D. (2007). 10 unsolved mysteries of the brain: What we know—and don't know—about how we think. *Discover, 28*(8), 54–59, 75.

Edwards, P.A. (2007, December). *The Education of African American students: Voicing the debates, controversies, and solutions.* Presidential address to the National Reading Conference, Austin, TX.

Ericsson, K.A., & Kintsch, W. (1995). Long-term working memory. *Psychological Review, 102*(2), 211–245. doi:10.1037/0033-295X.102.2.211

Fabbro, F. (2001). The bilingual brain: Cerebral representation of languages. *Brain and Language, 79*(2), 211–222. doi:10.1006/brln.2001.2481

Fiez, J.A., & Petersen, S.E. (1998). Neuroimaging studies of word reading. *Proceedings of the National Academy of Sciences of the United States of America, 95*(3), 914–921. doi:10.1073/pnas.95.3.914

Fisher, D., & Frey, N. (2008a). *Better learning through structured teaching: A framework for the gradual release of responsibility.* Alexandria, VA: Association for Supervision and Curriculum Development.

Fisher, D., & Frey, N. (2008b). *Improving adolescent literacy: Content area strategies at work* (2nd ed.). Upper Saddle River, NJ: Pearson.

Fisher, D., & Frey, N. (2008c). What does it take to create skilled readers? Facilitating the transfer and application of literacy strategies. *Voices From the Middle, 15*(4), 16–22.

Fisher, D., Frey, N., & Lapp, D. (2008). Shared reading: Modeling comprehension, vocabulary, text structures, and text features for older readers. *The Reading Teacher, 61*(7), 548–556.

Frey, N., Fisher, D., & Berkin, A. (2009). *Good habits, great readers: Building the literacy community.* Upper Saddle River, NJ. Pearson.

Frey, N., Fisher, D., & Hernandez, T. (2003). What's the gist? Summary writing for struggling adolescent writers. *Voices From the Middle, 11*(2), 43–49.

Graves, M.F., & Slater, W.H. (1996). Vocabulary instruction in content areas. In D. Lapp, J. Flood, & N. Farnan (Eds.), *Content area reading and learning: Instructional strategies* (2nd ed., pp. 261–276). Boston: Allyn & Bacon.

Guthrie, J.T., Van Meter, P., McCann, A.D., Wigfield, A., Bennett, L., Poundstone, C.C., et al. (1996). Growth of literacy engagement: Changes in motivations and strategies during concept-oriented reading instruction. *Reading Research Quarterly, 31*(3), 306–332. doi:10.1598/RRQ.31.3.5

Guthrie, J.T., & Wigfield, A. (2000). Engagement and motivation in reading. In M.L. Kamil, P.B. Mosenthal, P.D. Pearson, & R. Barr (Eds.), *Handbook of reading research* (Vol. 3, pp. 403–424). Mahwah, NJ: Erlbaum.

Hart, B., & Risley, T.R. (1995). *Meaningful differences in the everyday experience of young American children.* Baltimore: Paul H. Brookes.

Harvey, S., & Goudvis, A. (2000). *Strategies that work: Teaching comprehension to enhance understanding.* York, ME: Stenhouse.

Hawkins, J., & Blakeslee, S. (2004). *On intelligence.* New York: Times Books.

Hebb, D.O. (1949). *The organization of behavior: A neuropsychological theory.* New York: Wiley.

Heffernan, N. (2003). Building a successful TOEFL program: A case study. *Language Teaching, 27*(8), 2–8.

Herber, H.L. (1978). *Teaching reading in the content areas* (2nd ed.). New York: Prentice Hall.

Herman, P.A., Anderson, R.C., Pearson, P.D., & Nagy, W.E. (1987). Incidental acquisition of word meaning from expositions with varied text features. *Reading Research Quarterly, 22*(3), 263–284. doi:10.2307/747968

Holdaway, D. (1979). *The foundations of literacy.* Sydney: Ashton Scholastic.

Holdaway, D. (1983). Shared book experience: Teaching reading using favorite books. *Theory Into Practice, 21*(4), 293–300.

Hurley, S.L. (2008). The shared circuits model. How control, mirroring, and simulation can enable imitation, deliberation, and mindreading. *Behavioral and Brain Sciences, 31(1), 1–22.*

Hymes, D. (1981). Foreword. In. C.A. Ferguson & S.B. Heath (Eds.), *Language in the USA* (pp. v–ix). New York: Cambridge University Press.

Keene, E.O., & Zimmermann, S. (1997). *Mosaic of thought: Teaching comprehension in a reader's workshop.* Portsmouth, NH: Heinemann.

Kintsch, W. (1988). The role of knowledge in discourse comprehension: A construction-integration model. *Psychological Review, 95*(2), 163–182. doi:10.1037/0033-295X.95.2.163

Kobayashi, M. (2002). Method effects on reading comprehension test performance: Text organization and response format. *Language Testing, 19*(2), 193–220. doi:10.1191/0265532202lt227oa

Koch, C. (2005). The movie in your head. *Scientific American.* Retrieved November 23, 2007, from www.sciam.com/article.cfm?id=the-movie-in-your-head&print=true

LaBerge, D., & Samuels, S.J. (1974). Toward a theory of automatic information processing in reading. *Cognitive Psychology, 6*(2), 293–323. doi:10.1016/0010-0285(74)90015-2

Landlaw, J., & Bodian, S. (2003). *Buddhism for dummies.* New York: Wiley.

Marzano, R.J. (2004). *Building background knowledge for academic achievement: Research on what works in schools.* Alexandria, VA: Association for Supervision and Curriculum Development.

Marzano, R.J., Pickering, E.J., & Pollock, J.E. (2001). *Classroom instruction that works: Research-based strategies for increasing student achievement.* Alexandria, VA: Association for Supervision and Curriculum Development.

McCloud, S. (1994). *Understanding comics: The invisible art.* New York: Harper.

McCrudden, M.T., Schraw, G., Lehman, S., & Poliquin, A. (2007). The effects of causal diagrams on text learning. *Contemporary Educational Psychology, 32*(3), 367–388. doi:10.1016/j.cedpsych.2005.11.002

McKeown, R.G., & Gentilucci, J.L. (2007). Think-aloud strategy: Metacognitive development and monitoring comprehension in the middle school second-language classroom. *Journal of Adolescent & Adult Literacy, 51*(2), 136–147. doi:10.1598/JAAL.51.2.5

McKoon, G., & Ratcliff, R. (1992). Inference during reading. *Psychological Review, 99*(3), 440–466. doi:10.1037/0033-295X.99.3.440

McMackin, M.C., & Witherell, N.L. (2005). Different routes to the same destination: Drawing conclusions with tiered graphic organizers. *The Reading Teacher, 59*(3), 242–252. doi:10.1598/RT.59.3.4

McNamara, D.S., & Kintsch, W. (1996). Learning from texts: Effects of prior knowledge and text coherence. *Discourse Processes, 22*(3), 247–288.

McNay, M., & Melville, K.W. (1993). Children's skill in making predictions and their understanding of what predicting means: A developmental study. *Journal of Research in Science Teaching, 30*(6), 561–577.

Medina, J. (2008). *Brain rules: 12 principles for surviving and thriving at work, home, and school.* Seattle: Pear Press.

Meyer, B.J.F. (2003). Text coherence and readability. *Topics in Language Disorders, 23*(3), 204–224.

Miller, G.A. (1956). The magical number seven, plus or minus two: Some limits of our capacity for processing information. *Psychological Review, 63*(2), 81–97. doi:10.1037/h0043158

Miller, G.A. (2001). Ambigious words. Retrieved on November 12, 2007, from www.kurzweilai.net/meme/frame.html?main=/articles/art0186.html

Mosenthal, P.B., & Kirsch, I.S. (1992). Types of document knowledge: From structures to strategies. *Journal of Reading, 36*(1), 64–67.

Nagourney, E. (2007). *Aging: Flip side to education is seen in dementia.* Retrieved November 12, 2007, from www.nytimes.com/2007/11/06/health/research/06agin.html?ref=science

Nagy, W.E., & Anderson, R.C. (1984). How many words are there in printed school English? *Reading Research Quarterly, 19*(3), 304–330. doi:10.2307/747823

Nagy, W.E., Anderson, R.C., Herman, P.A. (1985). Learning words from context. *Reading Research Quarterly, 20*(2), 233–253.

Palincsar, A.S., & Brown, A.L. (1984). Reciprocal teaching of comprehension-fostering and comprehension-monitoring activities. *Cognition and Instruction, 1*(2), 117–175 doi:10.1207/s1532690xci0102_1

Palincsar, A.S., & Brown, A.L. (1986). Interactive teaching to promote independent learning from text. *The Reading Teacher, 39*(8), 771–777.

Paris, S.G., Wasik, B.A., & Turner, J.C. (1991). The development of strategic readers. In R. Barr, M.L. Kamil, P.B. Mosenthal, & P.D. Pearson (Eds.), *Handbook of reading research* (Vol. 2, pp. 609–640). New York: Longman.

Parsons, J. (2000). Helping students learn how textbooks are written. *Canadian Social Studies, 35*(1), 1–3.

Pearson, P.D., & Gallagher, G. (1983). The gradual release of responsibility model of instruction. *Contemporary Educational Psychology, 8*(3), 112–123.

Piaget, J. (1970). *The child's conception of movement and speed.* New York: Basic Books.

Pichert, J.W., & Anderson, R.C. (1977). Taking different perspectives on story. *Journal of Educational Psychology, 69*(4), 309–315. doi:10.1037/0022-0663.69.4.309

Potelle, H., & Rouet, J.-F. (2003). Effects of content representation and readers' prior knowledge on the comprehension of hypertext. *International Journal of Human–Computer Studies, 58*(3), 327–346. doi:10.1016/S1071-5819(03)00016-8

Pressley, M. (2002a). Comprehension strategies instruction: A turn-of-the-century status report. In C.C. Block & M. Pressley (Eds.), *Comprehension instruction: Research-based best practices* (pp. 11–27). New York: Guilford.

Pressley, M. (2002b). Metacognition and self-regulated comprehension. In A.E. Farstrup & S.J. Samuels (Eds.), *What research has to say about reading instruction* (3rd ed., pp. 291–307). Newark, DE: International Reading Association.

Raphael, T.E., & Au, K.H. (2005). QAR: Enhancing comprehension and test taking across grades and content areas. *The Reading Teacher, 59*(3), 206–221. doi:10.1598/RT.59.3.1

Rinehart, S.D., Stahl, S.A., & Erickson, L.G. (1986). Some effects of summarization training on reading and studying. *Reading Research Quarterly, 21*(4), 422–438.

Rosenblatt, L.M. (1960). Literature: The reader's role. *English Journal, 49*(5), 304–310, 315, 316. doi:10.2307/810700

Rosenshine, B., & Meister, C. (1994). Reciprocal teaching: A review of the research. *Review of Educational Research, 64*(4), 479–530.

Sadoski, M., & Paivio, A. (2004). A dual coding theoretical model of reading. In R.B. Ruddell & N.J. Unrau (Eds.), *Theoretical models and processes of reading* (5th ed., pp. 1329–1362). Newark, DE: International Reading Association.

Sadoski, M., Paivio, A., & Goetz, E.T. (1991). A critique of schema theory in reading and a dual code alternative. *Reading Research Quarterly, 26*(4), 463–484. doi:10.2307/747898

Sanders, T. (1997). Semantic and pragmatic sources of coherence: On the categorization of coherence relations in context. *Discourse Processes, 24*(1), 119–148.

Short, R.A., Kane, M., & Peeling, T. (2000). Retooling the reading lesson: Matching the right tools to the job. *The Reading Teacher, 54*(3), 284–295.

Silani, G., Frith, U., Demonet, J.-F., Fazio, F., Perani, D., Price, C., et al. (2005). Brain abnormalities underlying altered activation in dyslexia: A voxel-based morphometry study. *Brain, 128*(10), 2453–2461. doi:10.1093/brain/awh579

Simpson, M.L., & Nist, S.L. (2000). An update on strategic learning: It's more than textbook reading strategies. *Journal of Adolescent & Adult Literacy, 43*(6), 528–541.

Skeans, S.S. (2000). Reading...with pen in hand! *English Journal, 89*(4), 69–72. doi:10.2307/821987

Squire, L.R., & Kandel, E.R. (2000). *Memory from mind to molecules.* New York: W.H. Freeman.

Surber, J.R., & Schroeder, M. (2007). Effect of prior domain knowledge and headings on processing of informational text. *Contemporary Educational Psychology, 32*(3), 485–498. doi:10.1016/j.cedpsych.2006.08.002

Swinney, D.A. (1979). Lexical access during sentence comprehension: (Re) considerations of context effects. *Journal of Verbal Learning and Verbal Behavior, 18*(6), 645–659.

Takaki, R.T. (2000). *Double victory: A multicultural history of America in World War II*. Boston: Little, Brown and Company.

Taylor, B.M., & Pearson, P.D. (Eds.). (2002). *Teaching reading: Effective schools, accomplished teachers*. Mahwah NJ: Erlbaum.

Taylor, J.B. (2006). *My stroke of insight: A brain scientist's personal journey*. Bloomington, IN: Author.

Tennyson, R.D., & Cocchiarella, M.J. (1986). An empirically based instructional design theory for teaching concepts. *Review of Educational Research, 56*(1), 40–71.

Thorndike, E.L. (1917). Reading as reasoning: A study of mistakes in paragraph reading. *Journal of Educational Psychology, 8*(6), 323–332. doi:10.1037/h0075325

Topping, K., & Ferguson, N. (2005). Effective literacy teaching behaviours. *Journal of Research in Reading, 28*(2), 125–143. doi:10.1111/j.1467-9817.2005.00258.x

Tovani, C. (2000). *I read it, but I don't get it: Comprehension strategies for adolescent readers*. Portland, ME: Stenhouse.

Tyree, R.B., Fiore, T.A., & Cook, R.A. (1994). Instructional materials for diverse learners. *Remedial and Special Education, 15*(6), 363–377.

University of California–San Diego. (2005, May 26). *Grasping Metaphors: UC San Diego researcher ties brain area to figure of speech*. Retrieved August 28, 2008, from ucsdnews.ucsd.edu/newsrel/general/RamaMetaphor.asp

Vacca, R.T., & Vacca, J.L. (1999). *Content area reading: Literacy and learning across the curriculum* (6th ed.). New York: Longman.

van den Broek, P., Fletcher, C.R., & Risden, K. (1993). Investigations of inferential processes in reading: A theoretical and methodological integration. *Discourse Processes, 16*(1–2), 169–180.

Vygotsky, L.S. (1986). *Thought and language* (A. Kozulin, Trans.). Cambridge, MA: MIT Press. (Original work published 1934)

Vygotsky, L.S. (1997). *The history of the development of higher mental functions*. (M.J. Hall, Trans.). New York: Plenum.

Wilhelm, J. (2001). *Improving comprehension with think-aloud strategies: Modeling what good readers do*. New York: Scholastic.

Willis, J. (2008). Building a bridge from neuroscience to the classroom. *Phi Delta Kappan, 89*(6), 424–427.

Winerman, L. (2005). The mind's mirror. *Monitor on Psychology, 36*(9). Retrieved June 25, 2008, from www.apa.org/monitor/oct05/mirror.html

Wolf, M. (2007). *Proust and the squid: The story and science of the reading brain*. New York: HarperCollins.

Wolfe, P. (2001). *Brain matters: Translating research into classroom practice*. Alexandria, VA: Association for Supervision and Curriculum Development.

Wolsey, T.D., & Fisher, D. (2008). *Learning to predict and predicting to learn: Cognitive strategies and instructional routines*. Boston: Allyn & Bacon.

Yang, Y. (2006). Reading strategies or comprehension monitoring strategies? *Reading Psychology, 27*(4), 313–343. doi:10.1080/02702710600846852

Literature Cited

Avi. (1986). *Wolf rider*. New York: Simon Pulse.

Bunting, E. (1997). *I am the Mummy Heb-Netert*. San Diego, CA: Harcourt.

Cisneros, S. (1991). *Woman hollering creek, and other stories*. New York: Vintage.

Eisner, W. (2000). *New York: The big city*. New York: DC Comics.

Frost, R. (1969). Stopping by woods on a snowy evening. In E.C. Lathem (Ed.), *The Poetry of Robert Frost* (p. 224). New York: Holt. (Original poem published 1923)

Hatkoff, I., Hatkoff, C., & Kahumbu, P. (2006). *Owen and Mzee: The true story of a remarkable friendship*. New York: Scholastic.

Hinton, S.E. (1967). *The outsiders*. New York: Viking.

Lehman, B. (2004). *The red book*. Boston: Houghton Mifflin.

Machiavelli, N. (1908). *The prince* (W.K. Marriotte, Trans.). New York: E.P. Dutton & Co.

Myers, W.D. (2002). *Patrol: An American soldier in Vietnam*. New York: HarperCollins.

Nash, O. (1945). The Germ. In *Many long years ago*. Retrieved July 24, 2008, from www.poemhunter.com/poem/the-germ/

Naylor, P.R. (1991). *Shiloh*. New York: Bantam Doubleday Dell.

Orwell, G. (1946). *Animal farm*. New York: Harcourt, Brace and Company.

Poe, E.A. (1994). *A collection of stories*. New York: Tor.

Ryan, P.M. (2000). *Esperanza rising*. New York: Scholastic.

White, E.B. (1952). *Charlotte's web*. New York: Harper.

Woodson, J. (2004). *Coming on home soon*. New York: Putnam.

Note: Page numbers followed by *f* and *t* indicate figures and tables, respectively.

I

J

K

L

Q

QUESTIONING STRATEGY, 45–47
QUESTIONS TO FACILITATE MAKING CONNECTIONS, 53*t*

R

RAMACHANDRAN, V.S., 58
RAPHAEL, T.E., 45
RATCLIFF, R., 40
READING: biological systems involved in, 14; with different perspectives, 113, 114*f*; self-regulated, 26–27; as skill to be taught, 15; as transaction, 54. *See also* shared reading; wide reading
RECIPROCAL TEACHING, 19–20, 120–121
REPETITION, AND LEARNING, 88
RESOURCES, FOR WORD SOLVING, 77–78
RINEHART, S.D., 42
RISDEN, K., 40
RISLEY, T.R., 61
RODGERS, L.L., 44
ROSENBLATT, L.M., 24–25, 27
ROSENSHINE, B., 19
ROUET, J.-F., 33
RYAN, P.M., 92

S

SADOSKI, M., 103
SAMUELS, S.J., 15
SANDERS, T., 82
SCHALLERT, D.L., 83
SCHEMA, 27, 28
SCHRAW, G., 104
SCHROEDER, M., 101
SECONDARY TEXTBOOKS, TEXT FEATURES IN, 102*t*
SELF-EFFICACY, AND MOTIVATION, 30
SELF-REGULATED READING, 26–27
SEMANTIC FEATURE ANALYSIS, 71, 71*f*
SENSORY-MOTOR CORTEX, 15
SHARED READING, 5, 6, 18*t*, 120–121
SHORT, R.A., 5
SIGNAL WORDS, 81, 88, 99
SILANI, G., 58
SIMPSON, M.L., 83
SKEANS, S.S., 113
SLATER, W.H., 66
SMALL-GROUP GUIDED INSTRUCTION, 17–18
SMITH, E.E., 48
SOCIAL INTERACTION, AND LEARNING, 28, 31
SPECIALIZED VOCABULARY, 63
SQUIRE, L.R., 15
STAHL, S.A., 42
STANOVICH, K.E., 69

VOCABULARY: deep vocabulary instruction, 64–65; definition and subtypes of, 18*t*; experience, and acquisition of, 61; hard books and, 26; modeling, 118–119; specialized, 63; technical, 63–64; wide reading and, 29

VOCABULARY LEARNING. *See* word solving

VOEKL, K.E., 31

VYGOTSKY, L.S., 28, 31, 122

W

WASHINGTON, GEORGE, 49

WASIK, B.A., 27

WERNICKE'S AREA, 57, 58

WHEDON, C.K., 82

WHITE, E.B., 29

WHITFIELD-GABRIELI, S., 31

WIDE READING: vocabulary and, 29; word solving and, 68–70

WIGFIELD, A., 30, 31

WILHELM, J., 49

WILLIS, J., 7

WINERMAN, L., 16

WITHERELL, N.L., 40

WOLF, M., 12–13, 14, 24, 25, 26, 57, 57*f*, 77, 84

WOLF RIDER (AVI), 123–126

WOLFE, P., 14, 15, 17, 38

WOLSEY, T.D., 44

WOODSON, J., 72

WORD KNOWLEDGE, 55

WORD SOLVING: context clues, 72–75, 74*t*; modeling, 68; resources, 77–78; strategies for, 55–56; systematic approach to, 67–68; wide reading and, 68–70; word parts, 75, 76*t*, 77

WORDS: damage to brain and, 58; deep vocabulary instruction, 64–65; importance of, 60–62; inside-the-word strategies, 75, 76*t*, 77; instructional, choosing, 65–67; location of, in brain, 56–58, 57*f*; meaning of, 59–60; outside-the-word strategies, 72–75, 74*t*; types of, 62–64; working with, 70–72. *See also* word solving

WORKING MEMORY: definition of, 84; long-term, facilitating, 87–88; purpose of, 84–85; strategy instruction and, 37; text structure and, 85–87

WRITING SYSTEMS, HISTORY OF, 12, 13

Y

YANG, Y., 48

Z

ZIMMERMANN, S., 43, 53

ZONE OF PROXIMAL DEVELOPMENT, 28